Special
HIDDEN TALENTS

Special HIDDEN TALENTS

The Missing Link - Amadi's Story

*One mother's personal journey
through the world of special education needs*

CHINEME NOKE

Publisher:
Chineme Noke Consulting
www.chinemenokeconsulting.com

Publishing consultant:
Professional Woman Publishing
www.pwnbooks.com

ISBN: 978-1-9996795-0-7

Dedication

This book is dedicated to my beautiful daughter Amadi, the absolute brightest light of my life, who taught me that life is for living and not just for working.

Also to my dear, departed father – my absolute hero and sole support throughout this whole process, who taught me that self-belief and persistence is the key to achieving everything that means anything at all in your life.

Contents

Acknowledgements

I express my sincere appreciation to the team at the Professional Woman Network.

Thank you especially to Linda Ellis Eastman for providing this valuable opportunity for me to be able to spread awareness and provide such important support and encouragement to all advocates for our wonderful people with Special Hidden Talents.

Prologue

On the 1st November, 1998 I gave birth to a beautiful baby girl, whom I had already named Amadi Dara, in West London, United Kingdom. From my family's West African cultural background, Amadi means 'general rejoicing; happiness'. Dara is from East Africa and means 'the beautiful one'. From the moment I held my daughter in my arms and felt her energy, I knew that I had named her well. I am also gladdened that she chose to wait for All Saint's Day before her debut into the world.

My pregnancy – my first to full-term – was blissful. Granted, I gained over three stone in weight (mostly fluid retention that continued to flow throughout the whole night of my labour) but I felt healthier and happier than I had ever been. My friends, as well as random people that I met, frequently commented and complimented me on my glowing radiance throughout my pregnancy.

Amadi was very energetic from the first moment and I must confess to her almost falling out of my arms twice in those first few days in the hospital! On one occasion she toppled onto the soft, leather armchair beside my bed and I screamed in horror. Amadi however, never missed a beat and continued to slumber peacefully.

My 'labour' was a long one. Amadi was already 12 days 'overdue' when my waters broke and I was admitted into hospital. There then followed many overnight hours of induced labour but Amadi was clearly not ready to leave her warm, cosy development centre. Eventually, some fourteen hours later, I succumbed and requested the dreaded epidural since I could not cope with the fierceness of the induced contractions any longer.

However, no sooner had I relaxed back onto my hospital bed than the consultant overseeing our progress announced that Amadi was in distress and so had to "come out immediately." I burst into tears – my delivery had gone so far off from what her father and I had planned, that this seemed to be the final straw. Nevertheless, not even 15 minutes later, my beautiful bundle of joy was snuggling up on my breast and the surgeon was marvelling at what a fantastic job he had done in stitching up my Caesarean section. The photo of us at that moment, taken by Amadi's father, remains my ultimate treasure.

Amadi took to the breast immediately and loved to snuggle up onto my belly once she was satisfied. She curled herself up so tightly there that I often wondered whether she was trying to get back in! I gave birth to my only child relatively late in life and wondered whether every mother was as lucky as me. Did they share the same feelings of awe, wonderment and deep, deep gratitude to the Universe as I did from that day forth? I suppose they must have, but I felt so privileged that my beautiful creation had chosen me to be her birth mother.

Amadi weighed six pounds and thirteen ounces, was skinny and very long. There were a few respiratory issues in the hospital and the nurses took Amadi away from me on three separate occasions to clear her nose and respiratory tract so that she could breathe more easily. On each occasion, I felt a sense of loss so deep, so profound, that I thought my heart was going to break. And they had only taken her a few metres down the corridor! A huge sense of relief swept over me whenever she was returned to her rightful place within my arms.

Apart from the congestion and a slight puffiness around her eyes, my little princess had scored 10 out of 10 on her Apghar test and, despite the Caesarean delivery, we went home three days later.

Home was my studio apartment – my bachelorette pad in West London for the previous 7 years. It was now home to Amadi, her father and me, and all of Amadi's stuff, which literally took over all of the available space. Fortunately, we had been looking for a bigger house and were due to move to North-West of London within the following couple of months.

Apart from the mandatory sleep deprivation, due to Amadi apparently needing no sleep at all, things went relatively smoothly. That is, if one can call living on the edge of chaos smooth. I recall my midwife looking around my dishevelled apartment while I wearily consoled my increasingly demanding baby, and calmly stating that all would be a lot easier were I to develop some sort of routine. Routine?! I didn't know whether I was coming or going and she spoke of a routine. Nonetheless, when Amadi was 5 weeks old she gave me the brightest, most dazzling smile that I had ever seen, and I felt that all was right with the world.

With the assistance of a dear friend of mine, the packing began for our move to a bigger house. Then something awful happened. Amadi had been feeding very well and on the day before the move she wanted so much more than my depleted body could provide, and so I decided to top her up with some baby milk that had been given to me by my midwife.

Some hours later, Amadi's hands had swollen up like small balloons and her face was very red. She was very, very hot to the touch. She didn't cry and in fact did not look as though she was in any kind of discomfort, but I sure was. Her father drove us to the hospital of her birth where various tests were carried out on her, including drawing blood from her feet causing her to scream so hard that I too began to cry. The medical professionals could find no apparent reason for Amadi's swelling, despite us recounting everything that she had ingested during the preceding twenty-four hours. We were subsequently transferred by ambulance to another hospital where Amadi was admitted to the baby ward and I remained there with her.

There began a long process of prodding, poking, injecting and generally contorting my tiny baby's body, including performing a lumber puncture on her tiny frame, apparently to rule out meningitis. The medical professionals thought it best to perform these actions in my absence since, they assured me, it would be better for me and for Amadi. Each time they returned her to me she looked absolutely depleted and devoid of any energy. I could tell that she had cried her little lungs out while she had been away. She was placed on a drip and had antibiotics poured into her tiny body. Through all of this, my baby retained a strange sense of calm when she was with me and this in turn helped to calm my own wrangled nerves.

That was the beginning of the medical issues causing my baby and me to spend the best part of her childhood and teen years in and out of various hospital emergency departments and specialist consultant appointments. Thereafter, issues surrounding her education and learning also became a major factor…

Introduction

Prior to having my daughter, I had always wondered how it was possible for children to go through the school system and come out at the other end without being able to read and/or write. One hears of people whom have lived with, and even hidden, their lack of these (to my mind, fundamental) attributes well into their adult lives.

However, on navigating the mainstream school system with my own child, reality dawned. It became shockingly clear that it was actually disturbingly easy for children to drop through the net, get left behind, cover up their perceived difficulties, and effectively be excluded from the curriculum, despite their physical presence in the classroom.

Following my daughter's diagnosis of Williams Syndrome, a congenital, chromosomal disorder resulting in many and varied medical, physical and neurological health issues, one thing that was clear in my mind was that Amadi could and would learn to read despite her global developmental delays. I had learned that many educational psychologists were of the view that any child could learn so long as they had a teacher that understood their particular difficulties and had the processes, willingness and understanding to administer them effectively. This made perfect sense to me; after all, it is the case that the true meaning of 'teacher' is to **cause** the student to learn (Oxford English Dictionary).

I have found that it is not so much that the powers that be within the education system are oblivious to alternative methods of teaching our children, but more that, due to the constraints placed upon the service by a lack of resources, there is no political will to ensure that each child receives an appropriate education – despite clear legislation to ensure the contrary.

I happen to be a lawyer and so was very well prepared to take on the system if this became necessary in order to have Amadi's particular case openly debated and ruled upon all the way up to the Supreme Court if necessary. I want to encourage all parents of children with learning difficulties to become effective advocates by telling the story of our own very personal journey, in the hope that it will provide the inspiration needed to take on the education system for their child. The law clearly states that each child is entitled to a free and appropriate education according to their particular needs. However, for reasons of expediency, our children get herded through the mainstream system as though they were one homogenous group with the same aptitudes and proclivities for learning.

Please do not misunderstand my position – of course there have to be proper systems in place to ensure satisfaction for the majority of the population, but my position is that a proper focus needs to be placed on that sizeable minority who fall outside of the mainstream and who could become well-rounded, productive members of society were they given the chance through the appropriate provision of the basic tools of reading, writing and numeracy.

A lack of financial resources is merely an excuse and a poorly espoused one at that. The amount of money poured into our special schools is phenomenal, particularly when considered against the needs of many of the children placed within them which range from the severely physically and mentally disabled (for whom they are undoubtedly a God-send) to those whom may have learning difficulties that could be better served in an environment where they could be taught in a way that they understand and to which they could favourably respond, such as those with

Williams Syndrome, dyslexia, hyperlexia, Asperger's Syndrome, Down Syndrome, many on the autistic spectrum and so on.

I knew that our journey would not be simple. It is an arduous process which is not for the feint-hearted. However, there is a wealth of research conducted by scientists, academics and educational psychologists who have detailed the workings of the brain and the part played by the sensory cognitive function in the *process* of learning. While the education systems focus on the strategy-based model of teaching, it is the process of learning that has been found to be important for many people who are missing out on the wonderful world of learning simply because they are not being taught to read, write and count in a way that they can understand.

It is one thing to recognise the body of research; however, it is quite another translating it all into actionable measures which the powers that be are willing to incorporate into their very inflexible structures – if indeed there are any opportunities to make them aware of the findings at all.

My journey so far has been fraught with emotional challenges. I want to reach out to those of you whom have children with learning difficulties/disabilities so that you know that you are not alone. You have probably learned that, although the future remains unclear, the actions you take and the support you provide for your child during this arduous process will give them an enormous amount of self-confidence and allow them to excel to the best of their abilities.

My efforts have included the incorporation of a charitable organisation, Special Hidden Talents, formulated to spread awareness of these issues and to provide information and support to those who need it, as well as everyone else who will join us in connecting, plugging in and strengthening that missing link between education and learning for all of our children. The charity is to be launched as soon as resources allow.

This is Amadi's story, relayed by her mother to provide support, hope, understanding and encouragement to all affected by the issues involved.

CHAPTER ONE

Early Medical Indications

Despite the Doctor's convictions to the contrary, I knew that the swelling to Amadi's hands, ears and feet and her raging temperature were due to the baby's milk that I had given her earlier that day. The medical professionals appeared to suggest that such an allergy would produce a skin rash rather than swelling of her extremities and had suggested that she must have ingested something other than milk on that drama-filled day. Nevertheless, I knew what I knew and so fed Amadi only from my breast for the five days that we remained in the hospital.

After Amadi was discharged, we went straight into our new home, the move to which took place during our confinement in the hospital. Feeling extremely grateful for being able to avoid the added pressure and stresses of moving house, we settled into our new surroundings. As soon as I was able, I contacted my former GP who was until then unaware of all that had transpired (since it was my midwife with whom I'd had contact throughout my pregnancy).

I explained my fears concerning Amadi's reaction to the baby milk and my GP suggested soya milk should my own feed need topping up again. This I used, only to find that it went straight through Amadi and appeared to cause another raging fever. Amadi was taken again to the hospital and was again given antibiotics and her temperature was brought down. I contacted my GP once more and this time was given a prescription for a milk-free, soya-free baby feed which I hoped would provide Amadi with the sustenance she required, without incident, whenever she needed more than I could provide.

From about six weeks old, Amadi projectile vomited after each feed, whether it was from my breast or the bottle. She had already been labelled as 'failure to thrive' as she had gained only a tiny amount of weight since she was born. I remember our clinic appointments which I so looked forward to attending in the hope that Amadi had gained a few ounces since the last visit, only to be disappointed once more when told that she had gained nothing, or often had lost weight. I was at a loss as to why this was and wondered whether it was due to her erratic sleeping habits.

Amadi hardly slept during those first few months. And I do mean that literally. She would drink me dry and then scream and scream well into the night as though she were in tremendous pain. Due to her sensitivities it was difficult to give her any of the colic-reducing medications since the ones that I could find all contained some form of lactose. This in turn meant that I was constantly extremely tired. Her father had taken to sleeping downstairs on the couch so that at least one of us remained sane during that difficult period.

There were many instances of Amadi being taken to the hospital due to a very high fever, now for no apparent reason. I took great care to ensure that she was given no milk or dairy products yet Amadi continued to get these sudden increases in temperature where her skin would be burning to the touch and she would appear very poorly indeed. We became very well- known at the local hospital and at our new GPs surgery at which I registered once we had settled into our new home.

In a bid to get to the root cause of Amadi's afflictions, our new GP was gracious enough to allow me to explore matters further by making referrals to various paediatricians specialising in differing aspects of child development. I much later discovered that my GP actually had me down as being rather neurotic but trusted my instincts enough to assist me in my quest to find out what it was that was ailing my dear child.

And so our lives continued with regular appointments at many hospitals checking Amadi's heart, lungs, liver, stomach, eyes, ears, reflexes, and any other vital organ and bodily function. To my GPs surprise, each investigation raised additional issues – Amadi had pulmonary stenosis which caused a heart murmur and so had to be closely monitored to ensure no deterioration of her heart ventricles. Amadi's natural calcium levels were very high and the reason for her body rejecting the dairy-related products (I later discovered that the condition was initially referred to as Hypocalcaemia due to the elevated calcium levels). Amadi's stomach was at times very hard and so constipation as well as colic was suspected, the pain from which was clearly the reason for her piercing screams and inconsolable nature during the night. Amadi suffered from severe reflux which made it difficult for her to digest food and was the cause of the projectile vomiting. Amadi suffered from hyperacusis, a condition affecting the noise receptors in the ears and this is what caused her to jump startled whenever she heard so much as the rustling of a sweet wrapper – all sounds were very much amplified for her. Amadi had visio-spacial and consequent balancing problems which meant that it was difficult for her to judge distance and textures. Amadi had related coordination issues as well as fine and gross motor deficiencies also related to low muscle tone. The list went on and on and on.

CHAPTER TWO

Bumpy First Nursery Steps

Our appointments and check-ups at these medical establishments continued with no diagnosis as to what particular condition that Amadi had. As the sole earner, I had to return to work full-time when Amadi was six months old and so she was placed in a day care nursery since her father claimed that he could not take care of her. I was very fortunate to find a nursery fairly close to home and on the route to my work place although it was extremely costly. The staff however was caring and particularly loving towards Amadi so at least I could rest easy about her well-being. Amadi was just nine months old when my relationship with her father came to an end, due in large measure to his total refusal and apparent inability to accept any responsibility for her care or well-being, and his increasingly violent behaviour towards me. From that day on, Amadi and I struggled on with our difficult lives by ourselves.

Given our constant medical appointments, I had to take a considerable amount of time out of work and was fortunate indeed to have had two very understanding managers who were also fathers and whom displayed an inordinate amount of empathy and understanding to Amadi's plight. They enabled me to conduct some of my work from home at times when I could not be in the office. The team members that I managed were also very understanding and were happy to contact me by phone whenever the need arose. I remain eternally grateful to Mike, Terry and my wonderful staff at Hounslow who provided support over and above their call of duty, especially when I needed to take even more time off to attend court proceedings to obtain an emergency injunction against Amadi's father.

Amadi's physical development was slow but steady and through it all she displayed that wonderful smile first shown to me at just five weeks old. Wherever we went, Amadi drew people towards her with her extremely friendly demeanour. Although pulling herself up by grabbing onto the settee (or anything else that would take her weight), Amadi did not properly crawl until she was 13 months old. This I learned from an excited call from one of her carers at the nursery! When I arrived to collect her later that day, I was overwhelmed with pride and joy as Amadi waddled towards me on her hands and knees.

Her first steps came some four months later with the encouragement of one of her Godfathers. Eddie stood her up and with great concentration she put one foot in front of the other. As Eddie caught my attention, I screamed with joy but this startled Amadi and she toppled over! It was several more months of trial and error before Amadi could claim to be a true walker.

Some months after Amadi began to crawl, there was a change in personnel in the nursery which had until then served us so well. I arrived to collect Amadi as usual one evening and there was a lump the size of a golf ball on her forehead.

She seemed very withdrawn and I asked with horror what had happened to her. One of the new members of staff explained that Amadi had had an accident but that she was ok. She then proceeded to wave her index finger in front of Amadi's eyes and said, "Yes, she's ok." I demanded a full explanation of what exactly had transpired to cause such an injury to one so young. It appears that Amadi – who could not yet walk – was placed on a tricycle and pushed by another child. She went straight into a brick wall and was propelled forwards, hitting her head against the said wall. The calmness with which this story was relayed to me was quite frightening. No medical assistance was sought – Amadi could well have been concussed by this trauma to her head but there was absolutely no concern shown by the nursery workers. So incensed was I by this state of affairs that I removed Amadi from the nursery that evening and never took her back. I wrote to the manager of the nursery expressing my disgust at firstly, the lack of supervision of these tiny children, and secondly to the manner in which my daughter's injury was dealt – they had not bothered to call me so that I could have her medically checked over since they had not thought it necessary to do so. Given that whenever she had so much as a sniffle I was called to collect her, this made no sense to me at all.

I received a written apology from the nursery manager along with a request for payment until the end of that month! I asked them to sue me so that I could counterclaim for negligence against them. I heard nothing further from them.

This of course left me in a bit of a practical dilemma in that I needed to make alternative care arrangements for Amadi in order to be able to continue working at my job. Fortunately, I was able to enlist the services of a local childminder for part of the week and a distant relative for the remainder while I searched for a more permanent solution. This came when I was introduced to another day care centre that was just a little farther away. The manager at this centre happened to be a parent of a child with special needs and so had an insight about the extra special care and supervision that Amadi required as did all of the nursery staff. My mind was put at rest once again.

CHAPTER THREE

Discoveries and Diagnoses

When Amadi was 18 months old she experienced her first international trip when I took her to Atlanta, Georgia to visit a good friend of mine. Given her sensitivities, one large suitcase was devoted entirely to her dairy-free milk, hypo-allergenic toiletries and as much kosher bread and other bits and pieces as I could muster, as recommended by a wonderful Jewish nurse at our GPs surgery. I worried about insect bites but was pleasantly surprised to discover that her sun-block also worked as an effective insect repellent. She continued to spread laughter and joy wherever we went and that first holiday for Amadi continues to provide a source of wonderful memories for me.

I will never forget that first aeroplane journey I experienced with Amadi. I was rather nervous about coping with all of the luggage and Amadi in her stroller as she was not yet walking. However, I did not need to have worried at all as the fantastic crew on her first flight could not have been more helpful. Even during the journey, Amadi made such an impression on the flight staff that I hardly saw her for the entire eight hour flight! That is the effect that Amadi had on everyone that she came into contact with. I managed to sleep more on that flight than I had done in one session throughout Amadi's life to that point! So taken was I by the generosity of the flight crew that I made it a point to write to them expressing my heartfelt gratitude to that particular crew on my return. I received a formal acknowledgement from them and sincerely hoped that my thanks was passed on to the crew in question.

On Wednesday 11th July, 2001 when Amadi was just over two and a half years old, we attended a general paediatric appointment at our local clinic. We met with a consultant whom we had not seen before and he spent a couple of hours speaking with me, interacting with Amadi, and generally taking so much more of an interest in Amadi's condition than I had experienced by any medical professional at any time before then. He made a lot of notes on his notepad, told me he would be in touch with my GP and then left the room to arrange a further appointment. I took the opportunity to sneak a peek at his notepad and saw the words, "Williams Syndrome?" I had intended to go on to work but after dropping Amadi off at her day care, I rushed back home and got onto the internet to find out what this could possibly have meant. The following is a diary entry that I made on a fellow parent's American website two days later:

"Chineme Noke on Friday, July 13, 2001 at 21:30:13
WS: Yes – Relation: Parent
Found: Link from a WS site – Which: UK WS Foundation
Comments: My daughter is 2 and a half and I have in the last couple of days put a name to her condition. Like many other parents, from the time of her birth I have pushed and pushed for tests on every aspect of what appeared to the medical professionals to be

seemingly unrelated ailments. At last we found a doctor who took the time to put everything together. I read his notes and saw he had written down WS. He has not yet told me this but I did my own research on the web. The relief to finally put a name to the 'symptoms' was immense, as was the feeling of total helplessness and devastation. I'm crying a lot. Really out of frustration. I'd like to thank your family so much for taking the time to share. Also all your guests. I don't feel so isolated now. As with others, my beautiful daughter is a bundle of joy and laughter with whom no one can help but fall totally in love. Much love and happiness."

Thus, I now had a name for my daughter's condition. It was a great relief to find out and know what she had because I could then tap into the body of knowledge available to provide her with the assistance she needed to get on with her life with as little discomfort as possible. At the same time, with that knowledge came the realization that there was no going back. Amadi's condition is congenital – chromosomal – there is no cure, just coping strategies. So rare was the condition then that very few people we encountered, including our medical professionals and GP, had ever heard of it. We never met that consultant again – he was apparently a locum filling in for someone else. Once again, I was full of gratitude, this time because of that very caring and thorough consultant coming into our lives at the time when he did.

After the diagnosis, I began learning as much as possible about my daughter's condition. I became a member of the Williams Syndrome Foundation in the UK (WSF) and the Williams Syndrome Organization based in the US (WSO). The WSO have an invaluable internet-based list serve where parents and others with an interest in WS connect with each other by email. This is no less than a God-send. I quickly introduced myself and asked for the experiences of others and their practical day-to-day issues. It was quite amazing to me to see the similarities in the facial features of those with WS and the commonalities so far as their personalities were concerned.

Like Amadi, other parents told of their children's loving nature and bright, sunny demeanor. They spoke of their friendliness and ability to engage all types of people wherever they went. They recounted the very difficult early times when there was a profound lack of sleep, colic, reflux and projectile vomiting, sensitivities to noise, balance and coordination difficulties and many other ailments, some from which we were clearly very lucky to have escaped relatively more lightly. The very worst for me were the stories of the chronic heart complications that had taken the lives of many WS children at or soon after birth. Many more suffered instances of invasive open heart surgery which claimed the lives of some of these children. Other health issues concerned the malformed digestive systems which meant that many WS children had to be fed through tubes inserted into their trachea. Some required heel cord surgery to prevent toe-walking and the subsequent problems caused by tight heel muscles and thin bone density.

The low muscle tone and bone density issues were the cause of many instances of bone fractures on falling over. Many WS children are wheelchair-bound. Late walking and talking was almost universal as was the love of music and natural rhythm that our WS children have. I was also able to get an insight into the kind of lives lived by adults with WS. Again this varied enormously. Most adults appeared to be able to live in sheltered or warden-controlled communities where they could live as much of an independent life as they chose depending on the severity of their symptoms. Many continued to reside with parents or relatives well into their adult lives. A few that I came across managed to live completely independently with the availability of assistance should they require it.

There is one very inspirational woman with WS who had no idea that this was what her condition was until she had a son who was diagnosed with the condition. It was suspected due to the heart problems with which he had been born. She told of how she was always labeled 'mentally retarded' through her school years and, although late, she had managed to learn to read and write once she had left the school system. She drives a car. She cares for her young son with all necessary assistance. Knowing about what is possible for Amadi gave me much hope for her future. One thing that is almost certain is that those with WS have a 2:1 chance of having a child with the condition. Nobody that I know of has known of any WS adult giving birth to a child who doesn't also have the condition.

Given the scant knowledge and experience among medical professionals that Amadi and I encountered, the international list serve was invaluable. Any of us could post a practical question about how to deal with any issues arising with our children and would get a flood of responses telling of other experiences and how the matters were dealt with. Also, whenever one of our children reached a milestone or overcame a previous obstacle, we all rejoiced as though they were our own. It gave me a feeling of belonging to a global family with members who cared so much about each other due to the common bond that we had in our children, that the lack of such feelings within our own families was not so bad after all. There were many, many stories of those nearest and dearest to the families with WS children either pretending that nothing was wrong or avoiding them completely. Blame played a huge role. There was much finger pointing and blaming one or other of the parents for 'causing' the WS in their children. Ignorance is quite literally bliss for these people who would rather be defensive and offensive rather than lend a helping hand. Life however had to go on for every single one of us parents and we got on with it, supporting one another along the way.

CHAPTER FOUR

Children's Social Services

Having finally obtained a diagnosis for Amadi's condition, this resulted in a Social Worker from the local Authority being dispatched to our home to ascertain how we were living and coping. Since Amadi now had an "official disability," it meant that she was entitled to attend a State nursery, free of charge! This was a great source of relief for me since we were by then borderline destitute with the threat of losing our home. The money paid out for her daycare could now be refocused on paying off my mounting debts and to pay for a local child minder to collect Amadi for me and look after her until I returned from work. The Social Worker was a true blessing in that she looked into other ways that I could be assisted with Amadi since I was a sole parent of a child with many challenges and no support, yet striving to hold down a demanding job. She managed to secure transportation for Amadi to and from the nursery, but in the absence of any close relative able to assist until I returned from work, this could not be taken up. This angel in disguise also managed to put me forward for an annual allocation of weekly respite care for Amadi to provide both her and me with infrequent breaks but, due to the constraints on the service, this was never available to us until over a decade later.

Once Amadi had settled happily within her new nursery I telephoned Social Services to speak with this Social Worker, only to be told that she had only held a locum placement and had left the Council's employ. For a good 10 years after, we never received any further assistance from social services. This made me wonder whether it was just the locum workers whom are able to take the time to find out about the people with whom they deal, while the permanent staff appears to totally disappear behind their processes and structures, within an over-whelming amount of paperwork for which they are responsible.

Nevertheless, our lives had been made relatively easier by the actions of that Social Worker and Amadi was now receiving occupational, physical and speech therapy to assist with her general development. As Amadi's fourth birthday approached, she was due to be assessed for educational purposes as a direct result of being placed in the nursery. However, after waiting several months and hearing nothing, I contacted the local education authority to enquire as to when the so-called statutory assessment was going to be taking place. To my utter astonishment, I was informed rather tersely that no such formal assessment was going to take place as, "there is nothing wrong with her" (referring to Amadi).

I reminded this rather over-officious official of my daughter's diagnosis and the myriad interventions she had had to endure as a result of her global developmental delays, but was informed that an officer had met with Amadi at the nursery and had decided that she did not require the statutory assessment. Upon what basis this 'decision' was made was not made clear to me (given the overwhelming weight of evidence to the contrary, it beggared belief) and so there began my very first battle – fighting for 'the system' to assess my daughter in accordance with their very clear legal duty to do so in order to ascertain the level of special assistance she may require when she begins her formal education. The legislation defines *special educational provision* as that which is additional to, or otherwise different from, the educational provision made generally for children of the same age.

It has always seemed rather odd to me that, despite a very well thought out education system based on legal rules and procedures, certain of the officials charged with the task of implementing the rules and policies seem hell bent on doing the precise opposite! I have a public sector legal background myself and I found it very rare indeed to find officers in authority that went about their daily work with enthusiasm and conviction. Indeed, I and people like me whom had determination, drive and commitment in the implementation of our public sector roles, appeared to me to be frowned upon and in fact vilified for wanting to make the difference that our roles should ideally typify.

It must be said that my legal experience and my knowledge of the workings of local government have been instrumental in my tenacity and determination to battle on for what my daughter very evidently required, and indeed for what the education laws state that she is entitled to receive. I am very well aware that behind the walls of bureaucracy there are normal individuals making and taking decisions that affect the very essence of our lives. Local government is what is termed 'a creature of statute' and what this means is that everything that it does must have a foundation in law. No one individual or body can take it upon themselves to make a decision that does not have a legal basis – all decisions must derive from one. Therefore, if the law is clear on a certain aspect of education, be it special or otherwise, it is not for any official to substitute their own understanding or belief for what the law states should or should not be the case.

CHAPTER FIVE

First School – Special Educational Needs

Given the body of ever-increasing professional reports concerning the level of Amadi's learning abilities (or indeed, lack of them), the local government officers could not maintain what I term their 'head-in-the-sand' stance for very long. I was eventually notified that the statutory assessment would indeed be taking place and, if found to be necessary, a Statement of Special Educational Needs (SEN) would follow as is indeed the legal requirement. A SEN is required by law where the local education authority is satisfied that a child within its area requires additional educational provision to what is normally provided, and it must set out what that provision will be.

It was made clear by all involved agencies, including the Council's own Educational Psychologist, that Amadi would require ongoing assistance in most areas; therefore, the assessment concluded that which was already evident to all concerned. This conclusion should have triggered the need for a SEN but again nothing at all was started until I contacted the Council to remind them that Amadi was due to begin her primary education later that year. I nonetheless began looking at mainstream schools within our general area to ascertain what, if anything, was provided by way of services for children with special needs. I researched the OFSTED (the Office for Standards in Education, Children's Services and Skills) reports of two particular primary schools before applying to each of them.

The first school we were invited to look at was a church school that I had been told had a few autistic children among their cohort and so I surmised that they must have had workable systems in place to cater for children of differing abilities. Throughout the meeting, the rather aloof Head teacher kept on glancing at Amadi in a rather peculiar way. I had explained what Amadi's particular issues were but I suspected that she half expected Amadi to do something, anything, to validate her special needs label. Amadi merely smiled brightly and continued to look through the picture book that she had taken from a shelf.

A few days later I received a letter stating that the school would not be able to offer Amadi a place because they had reached their quota but that she would be kept on a waiting list so that if another child declined their place Amadi would be in with a chance. I was not surprised to have heard nothing further from them.

The second school we looked at had an altogether different feel about it. There was warmth and a general feeling of well-being on entering the premises, and the Deputy Head whom 'interviewed' us was friendly and down to earth. She chatted to Amadi in a perfectly normal fashion and I could see that Amadi felt at ease with her. As the meeting came to a close I volunteered the fact that Amadi had some special issues and I could see that this had not been a factor in the deliberations. A few days later I received a letter offering Amadi a place at the school which I was very pleased indeed to accept.

Having secured a school place for Amadi meant that the part of the SEN process concerning identification of a school was quite straightforward as they could merely name her new school as the 'Appropriate School' for Amadi. So far, so good. There then came the question of additional support for Amadi within this mainstream school which, although it had its own speech and language unit, could not be expected to provide Amadi with the additional learning support that she undoubtedly required.

A SEN must include details of the special educational provision which the authority considers appropriate to meet the needs of Amadi and objectives of the actual statement. Given Amadi's visio-spacial, balance and co-ordination issues, it was clear that Amadi would require adult assistance in navigating her way around the school buildings and the playground. Amadi also had considerable attention and focus issues which meant that she required assistance to be kept on task in the classroom.

It is to be remembered that the whole special education ethos within the legislation is centered on children being educated within mainstream schools along with the appropriate additional assistance, unless the parent wishes their child to attend a special school. This is known as the policy of 'inclusion'. The cost of ensuring appropriate assistance in a mainstream setting pales into insignificance when compared to the cost of a place at a special school. Further, I know of no special schools within the state sector that teach children like Amadi in the way that they need to be taught in order to learn. Special schools have smaller groups of children who are taught the same strategy-based way, only slower. This method does not address the sensory-cognitive issues so crucial for children with Amadi's type of learning needs. Therefore, the pace at which they teach within the special schools makes absolutely no difference to these children whom might as well be trying to comprehend a totally alien language to their own.

It is the case that the reports used for the SEN, and indeed which formed part of the SEN, were very detailed in the needs identified and the objectives to be attained. However, an arbitrary figure seemed to have been plucked from nowhere and inserted within the SEN as the required hours of learning support that Amadi needed. It amounted to less than half of the school day. When I enquired as to how Amadi, and indeed her teacher and classmates, was expected to cope for the rest of the day, the authority asserted that the rest of the provision would have to be provided from the school's own 'delegated budget'.

The school informed me that this was not possible as their budget was targeted for their special unit and others not necessarily with statements. This seemed like a very sensible assertion and, given the authority's blanket refusal despite my appeals to look further into what I also believed was their responsibility, I instituted formal proceedings in the Special Educational Needs and Disability Tribunal (SENDIST) in accordance with the legal procedure.

I ensured that my legal research was thorough. I set out the law as well as the factual circumstances of Amadi's case to date. This included recounting an incident where a relief teacher, clearly unaware of the situation, had taken over Amadi's class for a day but within minutes of starting, an accident occurred where a young boy tripped and stumbled into Amadi who lost her footing and had fallen against a table that hit another child who fell and banged her head on the floor. Amadi had a split lip and bleeding gums. It is my belief that this situation was made so much worse because Amadi was unsupervised and her balance and coordination issues came into play.

A few days after the submission of my lengthy case, I was informed that the authority was no longer going to contest the case or oppose my request and that Amadi would be provided with adult support throughout the school day after all. To my mind, this was necessary for Amadi, the teachers and the other children.

CHAPTER SIX

The School's Governing Body

During Amadi's reception year, a position for a Parent Governor came up and I decided to apply in order to do my bit for the school and indeed the community in general. It was of course an unpaid, voluntary position and the meetings were held in the early evening. I was very impressed with how the school was run and the commitment of the staff in working together to fulfill the 'corporate vision', led very effectively by the Head teacher. The only area that caused me some concern was that regarding the pupils with special educational needs. While they were undoubtedly well cared for, there appeared to me to be no aspirations as far as they were concerned. They were not included in any school test results or scoring of any kind. Apart from their physical number they were, to my mind, invisible to the school governors.

Given that we were now some three years down the road from Amadi's diagnosis, I had acquired a great deal of knowledge concerning her particular condition and, indeed, lots of general information concerning the workings of the brain and the part cognition played in our ability to learn. Fascinating stuff indeed. Stuff that I would have imagined would be equally fascinating to the State and the school system. In my experience however, it was not. Or at least there was no discernible interest in taking some necessary steps to ensure that the magic of learning was made possible for a great many more of the children within the education system. I could see that, for a straightforwardly stable and routine existence, relative certainty with the numbers in the majority can seem very much more attractive to an already overburdened system, than the relative uncertainty of introducing concepts to the minority of pupils whom may or may not benefit from some novel learning processes. Thus, easier then to just keep them safe and leave them be?

In my role as governor I made great efforts to bring awareness to the governing body about certain matters that affected the learning ability of certain children, my own included, and how there were ways in which to deal with these. This however was not something about which the Head teacher wanted to hear, and it was clear to me that the other governors also did not share my concern. I provided evidence to show that the type of sensory-cognitive processes that I spoke about helped all learners, not just those with learning challenges. Imagine, I postulated, the school's test results going through the roof simply because the whole pupil body was exposed to these innovative, yet tried and tested modes of teaching. After many months of being given the brush-off, I utilized the proper channels and wrote a paper on the subject and submitted it as an agenda item for the governing body to properly consider. However, this caused the Head teacher much consternation and it must be said that she was absolutely livid! I was scolded in front of the governing body and reprimanded for "exceeding (my) remit as a governor."

I was taken aback but not deterred. I was perfectly aware of my legal duties and responsibilities as a governor and I was in fact carrying them out in a perfectly correct manner! It is the case that school governors have a legal obligation to ensure that the children within their school whom have special educational needs are provided with the appropriate special educational provision that their particular learning difficulties require. For whatever reason, that certainly was not the case so far as Amadi was concerned. We governors are also legally obliged to ensure that the teachers within the school have identified and provided for these childrens' particular special educational needs. Again, this certainly was not the case with Amadi.

It is the case that Williams Syndrome is a condition that the school had never heard of and, despite my attempts to educate and spread awareness through information and written materials, there was no real will to understand the symptoms related to the conditions which are complex in the extreme. There is a pamphlet prepared by the Williams Syndrome Foundation which profiles the special educational needs for children with Williams Syndrome. Copies of this have been provided for the school and the local education authority. Within the first paragraph it states very clearly that, "...it's worth emphasizing that these children are not like other children with learning difficulties, they have *particular* needs." Thus, the trend of carting them off to special schools simply will not suffice. Indeed, I know that such a move would be detrimental to Amadi because she would then lose that social aspect of school ***as well as*** not being able to access the magic of learning.

The state system appears to treat all children with special educational needs as one homogenous group who has the same or very similar special educational needs. This in actual fact is contrary to law but, hey, who cares? I do. As do many parents of children with special educational needs who have their particular needs over-ridden for the sake of expediency and the channeling of the vast majority through its rigid, well-defined structures.

It was clear that I was not going to be gaining any support for my apparently novel ideas for raising the attainment levels of the school as a whole and so, my attention shifted from the general to the particular, i.e. my own daughter and her learning needs. My biggest and longest battles were yet to come.

CHAPTER SEVEN

An Appropriate Education?

Amadi's first year of primary school was what in the UK is termed the Reception year and we were blessed to have had a wonderful class teacher, who also happened to be the head of year. She recognized my own efforts in working systematically with Amadi out of school to ensure that she was able to understand matters raised within the classroom so that she did not feel at all left behind. It must be remembered that I am speaking of four to five year olds and so at that stage there was not too much of a gap so far as academic achievement was concerned.

As time went on however, the gap between Amadi and her peers grew wider and wider. At four to five, children are beginning to read and write. That was not the case for Amadi. She could recognize her own name and could sing the alphabet. But when it came to progressing from that level, it just did not happen. Thus, Amadi remained at the Reception stage level throughout year one, year two, year three and year four. By year one, I had begun to liaise with the school's Special Educational

Needs Coordinator (SENCO) about Amadi's particular difficulties and what I now knew she required in order to be able to learn. Although very sympathetic to Amadi's needs, it was made clear that the school was not prepared to, and indeed was not in a position to make any further provision for Amadi.

Over the years, the school had made various changes to personnel as far as Amadi's learning support went. As far as behavior is concerned, Amadi was very good at ascertaining how far she will be allowed to go before someone puts their foot down and says, "this far and no further." Indeed, any child worth their salt will experiment in this way. However, Amadi soon learned that her learning support assistants, as they were called, were in fact there just to keep an eye on her and were not in fact 'teachers' in the full sense of the word and so did not warrant the same level of respect and good behavior. I must say that there were many complaints made to me about Amadi's behavior towards her helpers and also some incidents of hitting and biting other children. This was totally unacceptable and I enquired as to where the support was at these crucial times. I was told in no uncertain terms that the support staff could not be expected to be with her at all times as there were other children who required their attention! This of course is despite the fact that they were employed specifically for Amadi's benefit in accordance with the SEN.

There was a total lack of understanding of the reasons why Amadi, who has always been a very bright child, would display such acts of frustration and even anger at seemingly innocuous events. I had an extremely difficult time trying to make the teachers understand that Amadi's frustration stemmed from wanting to learn as her peers were doing but being seemingly unable so to do. She simply could not understand what was going on around her and there was no effort made to ensure that she did learn in the only way that they'd been told that she could. As far as the school was concerned, they had done and were doing all that they possibly could for Amadi. They had changed her learning support to ones that she appeared to 'get on with' better. They had 'differentiated' the curriculum to what they considered she should be able to deal. They had even made it very clear that her lack of progress was down to me because I clearly could not have been taking her through her assigned homework!

It was increasingly impossible for me to get through to them the concept of Amadi's cognitive issues – the fact that her brain processes information in a different way to the accepted norm and that is the reason why she was not progressing, i.e. she simply did not understand what was being 'taught' because of the way in which it was being taught. The frustration associated with that simple fact was at the route of her disaffection. Despite the huge amount of information that I had provided to them, they simply would not allow for the differences in Amadi's cognition. The SENCO actually took me to one side and said, "Ah, but Chineme, we don't know how much of her behavior is down to Williams Syndrome, and how much is simply Amadi..." I was stunned into silence.

It became clear to me that more direct action was needed. Liaising with the teachers and the school SENCO was getting us absolutely nowhere. Annual individualized education plans (IEPs) were devised for Amadi on the basis of what the teachers in their professional experience considered was what Amadi required. The fact that she was not progressing one iota meant nothing – they were doing what they had always done and that was that. The "individualized" part of things was clearly an irrelevance to their procedures. I could feel the reluctance of the teachers to engage with me; I knew that I was becoming a thorn in their sides as I was clearly being unreasonable in expecting my daughter to actually *learn* at school, given her syndrome.

Amadi was effectively seen as a lost cause to them. My efforts to introduce a sensory-cognitive approach to learning to the school had failed. My efforts to encourage a teacher, perhaps the SENCO herself, to learn about the processes so that they could teach more of their pupils had also failed. I was however determined that my role as Amadi's advocate would not fail, no matter how much she was being failed by the education system. It is to be remembered that parents also have a legal duty to ensure that their children receive an appropriate education...

CHAPTER EIGHT

The Legal Statement of Educational Needs

As Amadi entered Year Four, I made a formal request for her formal Statement of SEN to be reviewed so that it could reflect more precisely what her special educational needs were. Despite the name of this legal document and the legislation behind it, neither the school nor the local education authority would engage with me on what Amadi actually required in order for her to learn.

There was an annual review meeting held at the school whereby all interested agencies were due to submit their reports on Amadi and attend the meeting. The only outside agency represented at the meeting was the Educational Psychologist (EP) who was in the employ of the local education authority. Also present were the school SENCO and Amadi's class teacher. I made clear my views on the lack of Amadi's progress. All agreed that the gap between Amadi and her contemporaries was getting wider and wider. All agreed that what had been done for Amadi thus far had not worked and was not working. The SENCO indicated that she did not know what else to do for Amadi. This was clearly despite everything that I had advocated for concerning the need for sensory- cognitive based learning instruction, but was instead based on *their* perceived views of the limitations on what she could achieve within the school setting.

I emphasized Amadi's learning needs again (as I had done for the previous four years) and the EP appeared to display some sympathy with my position. We discussed the Rudolph Steiner based model of teaching which also focuses on the sensory-language connection for learning, but there was not much knowledge about these schools which in any event were not local to us and were sparsely dispersed around the country. The EP did however include the essence of our discussions within her report which also made it clear that Amadi's progress at school remained under the Year One level.

I made a formal request that provision be made for Amadi to access a program that I knew about, had researched and had evidence of being of great benefit to other children with Williams Syndrome and those with many other learning difficulties. I re-emphasized that the law states that where an assessment reveals a special educational need "it is necessary for the local education authority to determine the special educational provision which any learning difficulty (Amadi) may have calls for, (and) the authority *shall* make and maintain" the statement of SEN accordingly. While a SEN had been made, it was very generalized in nature and did not make any provision at all for Amadi's particular learning needs, despite that being the whole point of the Statement.

There was no specification of the type of provision that Amadi needed for the purpose of meeting her needs as is required. The local education authority has the power to specify the type of school or other institution which they consider would be appropriate for Amadi. Four years prior, Amadi's school could have been considered appropriate but as time went on it was clear that there was another option which could be utilized, either in conjunction with the school, or as an alternative to it. The law provides for such circumstances by also referring to "other institutions" which may be appropriate for Amadi. Despite this, no other institution had even been countenanced despite my pleas.

Reports to the local education authority were also submitted by the Senior House Officer at the Primary Care Trust, the Speech and Language Therapist, the Occupational Therapist, and the Physiotherapist. No one could ever say that the fullest picture of Amadi and her needs were not exhaustively provided – the costs involved here were clearly not an issue for the education authority. All were clear that Amadi's learning fell far short of what it should be. The revised statement however merely restated all what the previous statement had recounted, the only difference being that it was noted that *"Amadi's school no longer had a place for her and some local special schools were now to be considered."* I was absolutely flabbergasted! No account had been taken of what Amadi required in order to be able to learn. It was once more just a matter of putting her somewhere, anywhere, so that her case could be closed and they could move on to other matters. Thus, the cost of all the professionals who had an input, in my view, were merely a waste of resources which could very easily have been re-directed towards the special educational provision that Amadi and others with learning difficulties very evidently required.

I took the opportunity to meet with the officer in charge of Amadi's case at the time at the Special Educational Needs Assessment Service within the local education authority. She listened to what I had to say and told me quite bluntly that the

Council "simply do not do" what I was requesting for Amadi, i.e. they were not prepared to do what the law states that they should do to provide for Amadi's SEN. I was told that Amadi's only option was to attend a 'special school' where she would be getting more time and attention. I again explained to this officer (whom incidentally informed me that she herself had a son who attended a special school) that no matter how slowly Amadi was taught, if it was in a language that she cannot understand, she will not learn. It certainly is not rocket science!

There then followed many months of correspondence wherein I pleaded for what Amadi required and provided details of a learning centre which provided for precisely the type of learning instruction that Amadi needed to be able to simply learn to read. I requested that Amadi be assessed by the centre to ensure that it was what she needed and that they could provide it. Everything I had to say fell on deaf ears. They were not interested and made no attempts to look into the learning centre in question or the model of learning instruction that it provided. Instead, I was provided with the names of a special school within the locality, and a 'special unit' attached to a school outside the locality, to which the authority had written requesting a place for Amadi! I was informed that if a place was available, that's where Amadi would be going. This, again, was despite the fact that there was clear evidence that she would not learn in those places.

I nonetheless proceeded to contact the Head Teachers of these schools and talked with them at length. I ascertained that, indeed, there were no special teaching methods save that the children were taught in smaller groups and were taught at a slower pace than within a mainstream setting. I made an appointment to attend at the special school within our locality and spent an afternoon with the Head teacher and another parent of a child on the autistic spectrum with attention deficit disorder. We were shown the facilities, classrooms and some of the children attending this splendid establishment. There was no doubt that no expense had been spared on the facilities within this school – there was even an indoor, heated swimming pool! Plus, to my utter delight, another girl with Williams Syndrome was in Year Six and had been attending the school for over five years.

We discussed our children with the Head teacher and in her opinion, she told us that she did not think the school would be beneficial for Amadi, although it sounded as though the other child would benefit there as his issues appeared to be mainly behavioral. I asked her specifically about the young pupil with Williams Syndrome and she showed me some of her work. This young girl was due to leave the school and enter her secondary education at the end of that year. She could not read or write. I agreed that Amadi's learning needs could not be met at that school.

I had satisfied myself that it clearly was not the special educational needs of Amadi that were being focused on when the referrals to these schools were made. Boxes clearly had to be ticked to show that the local educational authority was doing its job. It appeared to me, borne out by my experience, that they considered their job to be to place children in available schools. Tick them off the list. The objective of inclusion could be met by simply including them within the system – thus they were included; inclusion had been effected. Never mind about what these children with special educational needs actually *required* in order to learn. Never mind about the *resources* the schools required in order to simply teach them effectively.

There is clearly a great deal of public funds being poured into the special schools. Children attending them are very well looked after. The costs of funding a place for a child in these schools are considerably higher than placing them in mainstream settings, even with support. However, in Amadi's case it would not be beneficial because she would not be *learning*. Amadi has a great capacity for learning. I can confidently say that, having experience of the issues surrounding Williams Syndrome in particular, and I would hazard an educated guess at other learning difficulties that, were some of these funds put into learning centers that utilized the sensory cognitive model of instruction, placements at these special schools could be cut down at a stroke. The children who really needed to be placed within them would access what they required. The other children that had more of an issue with their inability to learn within the mainstream, strategy-based system could then benefit from specialist instruction that catered for their special learning requirements.

However, this type of logical reasoning does not appear to even be considered. It is not even contemplated when presented as an option in individual cases such as Amadi's. The special educational needs assessment service told me that they "simply did not do" this kind of thing. Amadi's school told me it was an impossibility to cater to Amadi's needs to the detriment of the rest of the pupils in the school. Why exactly it was considered a potential detriment to the other pupils was not elaborated upon. I had already presented the school and the education authority with research papers evidencing how a *whole school district* in the US had benefited from the sensory cognitive process of learning methods, so much so that their results outshone some of the more affluent and prestigious districts. I would wager that this paper remains unread. Certainly if it was looked at, it was simply disregarded.

CHAPTER NINE

Frustrations from Further Afield

I was turning into an emotional wreck. I knew this because whenever I received another of the nonchalant knock-backs from the education authority I would be in tears as I responded. I would be sobbing as I explained the situation to friends. My frustration at the total lack of care or understanding by the gatekeepers of the assessment of, and provision for, the special educational needs of my child and other children was taking its toll on my health. It was very difficult indeed to engage with this group of people who simply would not take on board anything that I had to say about Amadi's educational needs.

They simply were not assessing or making provision for my child in the way that their statutory roles state that they should. I had effectively done all of the homework, all of the research, and even provided them with documented evidence of what had been achieved by children who had had the benefit of the type of instruction required by Amadi and provided by this centre. All fell on deaf ears. The local education authority who were charged with the task of making provision for children in their area with *special* educational needs simply were not doing that in Amadi's case. They appeared to see their role as merely placing children within schools that would have them. There was absolutely no attempt to make any provision based on their actual educational needs.

Totally exasperated, I wrote to my local Member of Parliament (MP) to inform him of the situation and ascertain what, if any, assistance he could provide. I sincerely hoped that Amadi's plight could be raised at a higher level, as I was absolutely certain that there must have been a great many children nationally whose educational needs were being effectively ignored in the same way. My MP wrote to the local education authority restating my requests and also referred my concerns to the Secretary of State for children's affairs. To my dismay, the Government Minister eventually wrote back to me outlining the Statutory Assessment and SEN process as laid out by law. There was no appreciation, even by the person with national responsibility for these matters, that we had long since passed that stage. The current failings in the system that I had high-lighted were not even addressed.

I then turned to the UK's most prominent charitable organization for people with learning disabilities. I met their then Director at a business event and took the opportunity to speak with her about these ongoing issues and the difficulties I was having attempting to ensure that my local education authority provided Amadi with an appropriate education. I was kindly provided with the personal contact details of the person dealing with education policy matters at the organization. I contacted the relevant person at my earliest opportunity and relayed the whole sorry business to him. I asked what their position was surrounding this issue and whether there was any assistance that they could give me personally. Again to my dismay, I was informed that the charity did not have *any* policy surrounding the issues that I had raised. They were big advocates of inclusion. However, the *details* of inclusion for individual children, and indeed, the resources required to administer it effectively, had clearly not been their priority. The policy official with which I corresponded is now the organization's Director. I sincerely hope that the myth of inclusion will someday be addressed by them.

This knowledge spurred me on to found and register my own charitable organization, Special Hidden Talents. I was not going to leave this gaping hole in the nations education policies unplugged. I was absolutely determined that something had to be done about this missing link. Meanwhile, I had my own daughter's educational needs on which to concentrate. Amadi's learning needs were immediate. I knew that my fight for her would prove to be a fight for the greater good of other children and adults who were presently being ignored by the State education system. I had to push on with advocating for an appropriate education for my child.

One thing that became absolutely clear was the realization that I was on my own. I began to brace myself for the fact that the only avenue left open to me, should the situation not be dealt with effectively, was to take the matter to the law courts.

CHAPTER TEN

Unlawful Discrimination

While this debacle was ongoing, Amadi of course was still attending school. Although she was not learning in the conventional sense (i.e. to read and write) she did enjoy school for the social interaction with the other children there. She also benefited from the overall ethos of the school which advocated belief in self and respect for others. However, this too was shattered due to a thoroughly distasteful incident that occurred out of what was supposed to be a fun and enriching event.

The Parent Teacher Association at the school had organized a talent contest based loosely on shows such as the X Factor and American Idol. The children were to put themselves forward for group or sole performances in whichever field they chose. Some sang, some danced and some performed a combination of the two. The children were to go through a couple of elimination rounds before a core number performed in the finals which were to be the showcase at one of the school's family events.

Amadi, who just loves to sing and dance, was in a singing group with two other girls and I took the opportunity to sit in on the day that they had their particular round of heats. Out of about six acts, Amadi's group came in runner-up to a girl who performed a delightful dance routine. Therefore, Amadi's group was the top performing of all of the singing groups. At the end of all the heats a list of all the finalists was announced. The idea was to ensure that the top performing of all of the various acts performed in the finals. Amadi's group was not on the list. Another singing group was put forward instead – a group that was in the same heat as Amadi's group but had come in at fourth place on the day.

I enquired as to what had occurred for this to have happened – surely there must be some kind of mistake. Rather than answer my question, I was very rudely told that "parents should not have been in attendance at the heats." Taken aback, since the Chair of the Parent Teacher Association had invited me at the time to remain, I began to feel that something was definitely amiss. I wrote to the Deputy Head (who was in charge during a period of absence of the Head Teacher at another school). After much discussion amongst themselves, it transpired that the music teacher considered that Amadi should not perform in the finals because he didn't want to be faced with "any issues", and besides, he considered the group that he had put through would put on a better show!

This bombshell was relayed to me in a matter-of-fact manner by the deputy head who apologized to me and said it was the first time they had put on such an event and that they would do better next time. There was clearly no realization that what had happened was in breach of the Disability Discrimination Act not to mention common decency! So the one time that Amadi had achieved something special in her own right, on a level playing field with her peers, she was denied her rightful place for reasons of her having Williams Syndrome! I was so saddened and totally deflated because, up until that time, I sincerely believed that the school had been supportive of Amadi. Yet here was a time that she could shine but it was simply taken away from her.

I said nothing to the Deputy Head who clearly had no idea of the implications of what had occurred but I met with the SENCO and gently informed her that what the music teacher had done was unlawful. I wanted to find out whether there was any real understanding of what had been done. To my utter amazement she looked me straight in the eyes and said, "I know." She knew, but did nothing. The show went ahead with their hand-picked finalists, making a mockery of the process and breaking Amadi's heart – not to mention the feelings of her other two group members who also lost out through no fault of their own. I made the school aware of my disappointment at the way the matter was handled and pointed out that children of that age were being taught a very unpleasant lesson – compete to win but despite the result, you will be discriminated against. And, if your face fits, you can lose but still be wrongly chosen over those who do better than you. As a black woman in a very white male-dominated profession, I had come across these unwritten rules many times during my legal career. I considered it despicable that these little eight year olds had to come across them at the institution that was supposed to be teaching them right from wrong.

I left the matter there – needless to say, we did not attend the family event. The group that was wrongly asked to perform instead of Amadi's group did not win. At least some element of justice was done. However, knowing how the music teacher viewed my daughter ensured that I removed her from his extra-curricular music classes – I was not prepared to have to deal with "any issues" that may have arisen between them while he was in charge of the classes she was in. My confidence in the SENCO looking after Amadi's interests was shot to pieces.

CHAPTER ELEVEN

A Positive Step Forward

One afternoon before collecting Amadi, I went to meet with the SENCO to ask her about the local authority's assertion that the school no longer had a place for Amadi. She was not available and I directed my enquiry to the Head teacher instead. She was dismayed at the suggestion and assured me that Amadi would have a place at her school for as long as we wanted it! There had apparently been some miscommunication or misunderstanding between the SENCO and the local education authority. As far as the Head teacher was concerned, there was no need for the authority to be looking for other placements because Amadi already had a place there and she told me it would be there for as long as we wanted it.

Reassured by the school's support (or at least the support of the Head teacher whom until then appeared to be quite unaware of my attempts to obtain this method of learning for Amadi), I wrote to the authority again outlining what Amadi required by way of learning instruction, clarifying the fact that the school had not stated that they could not offer Amadi a place any longer and indicating that I was prepared to have Amadi's case legally reviewed if they continued to ignore her plight in the light of her educational needs. I stated that learning to read and write is surely a basic tenet of an appropriate education and I was utterly dumbfounded as to why they could not see this and provide her with what she needed to make this happen.

SENAS then informed me that they would be hiring a consultant to attend Amadi's school to provide advice as to how they can make accommodations for Amadi. I enquired what on earth would be the point? The hourly cost of the 'inclusion consultant', I knew from my local government days, would be phenomenal! Why, I asked, cannot the funds proposed for this futile move be diverted to my daughter's effective learning? They had previously indicated that educating Amadi in the way that I had proposed would not be an efficient use of their resources. I asked them if that meant that they considered it more cost effective for Amadi (and many others) to remain uneducated and a constant drain on State resources, rather than have them educated and become productive members of society? To date, I have received no response to these questions. Their actions until then however had spoken far more loudly than their words could ever have done.

I was fully aware that all documentation and correspondence between myself and SENAS would be available to a court should the matter proceed that far. I am pretty certain that they were also fully aware of this fact.

With the Head teacher's support, I was ecstatic to finally be given the go-ahead from SENAS to have Amadi evaluated at the learning centre that I had identified. I quickly arranged for Amadi to undertake an assessment at the centre and I also requested written confirmation about the educational needs of children with Williams Syndrome from the Williams Syndrome Foundation (WSF).

The assessment was a full diagnostic evaluation of Amadi's abilities and lasted approximately four hours. It was very thorough. Lo and behold, it confirmed what was already known, i.e. that Amadi could not read and write and that she was below the Year one level. They recommended an initial period of 10 to 12 weeks of intensive instruction to develop Amadi's concept imagery skills. This would then need to be followed by additional periods of instruction to develop reading, spelling, and mathematical computation skills.

I was absolutely delighted – six years at school and Amadi could not read or write. In a matter of months this could be remediated! How can anyone not be delighted and impressed with such news? Particularly the statutory agencies whose role it was to ensure that all children received an appropriate education? Not only the mainstream children, but those with special educational needs such as Amadi could actually be taught and could therefore become productive members of society instead of having to forever rely on the State. Are these not the objectives sought? Surely this type of information and knowledge is what the local education authority would be hungry for so that they have at least one more avenue to pursue in the pursuit of their statutory duties?

Similarly, the letter from the Chief Executive of the WSF confirmed the need for sensory-cognitive based learning processes and stressed the importance of phonemic awareness which underlies word identification skills, for people with Williams Syndrome as well as for those with other learning difficulties.

These documents were dispatched to the assessment service who informed me that due to staff holidays they would be dealt with in due course.

Sometime later, I received email correspondence from SENAS advising me that, with the approval of a senior officer and based on the "further information" submitted, they were prepared to follow the recommendations set out in the report which began with Amadi receiving 10 weeks of learning instruction at the learning centre. I was over the moon – because it was a start, the beginning of Amadi's journey to become a reader; Amadi was on her way. I refrained from dwelling on the fact that the "further information" merely confirmed all the previous documentation and information that I had already provided to SENAS over the years – this was a huge step forward, a huge, huge step. However, the emphasis on the "10 weeks" of instruction still stuck out like a sore thumb. Despite what the diagnostic learning evaluation had recommended, the authority had made a point of referring only to the initial concept imagery development period with nothing being said about the further reading and math work required.

CHAPTER TWELVE

Transition to Learning

Having received the go-ahead to at least begin Amadi's journey to becoming a reader, I launched myself into making all of the necessary arrangements with the learning centre as to Amadi's start date and the most appropriate daytime hours. We then had a period of about six weeks before Amadi's whole school routine would be totally revised. The centre was about five miles from our home and the instruction would be intensive for five days per week. I wanted Amadi to have as smooth a transition as possible given her tendency to become anxious at the thought of change.

I decided to take Amadi away with me on seminars that I had contemplated attending in order to acquire further enlightenment and learning for me and my business. The first one was in Los Angeles, USA and involved being on the panel of an Infomercial being produced by Dr. Ellie and Dr. Charlie Drake of Braveheart Productions. They also incorporated a two-day seminar about Passion Branding and how important it was to pursue one's passion with purpose, and how it could and should become one's livelihood given the all-encompassing nature of one's belief – one's reason for being. Given my belief and continued struggles concerning Amadi's education and the wider context of the system failing our children with learning disabilities, this was a salutary reminder (not that I required one!) and further motivation for me that we must not give up with pursuing something that we feel passionately about.

The other event was called "The Have It All Woman" in Toronto, Canada organized by Step Into Your Power Productions, run by life coach and entrepreneur, Susan Sly. The premise behind this event was that there is no reason why a woman must be limited in what she can accomplish should she desire it enough. It taught to reach out and work for whatever one's life purpose or desires are. The salutary lesson for me was to ask for what you want – if you do not ask, you will not get. As if by Divine intervention, the organization was also hosting their inaugural girl's event that year! The girl's event was meant to be for 11 to 17 year old girls but Amadi was allowed to attend given her particular circumstances and the fact that I would be there with her.

As is the procedure in these situations, Amadi's school required written notice that she would be out of school before the leave of absence could be formally authorized. I duly submitted the relevant form with details of the dates of travel. Our return date coincided with the school's half-term holiday which meant that upon our return Amadi would begin immediately at the learning centre. To my mind, the trip would provide a fantastic period of transition for her during which her confidence and self- esteem could be shored up prior to her, once again, having to emphasize her differences to her classmates by going for remedial reading instruction.

The school however did not share such apparently lofty ideas. I was initially told in no uncertain terms that if the school did not accept my absence request it could be recorded as unauthorized leave, which would deem Amadi to be a truant. This, apparently, could lead to me being pursued by the local education authority and the matter could ultimately end up in court! Blimey! Would that they acted with that much vigor when it came to Amadi's learning needs! I was told that it was a legal requirement that children are not to be out of school for holidays for more than two weeks in any academic year. Any more than that would have to be authorized. I restated my request for such authorization. This was not forthcoming. The Head teacher and the Deputy Head sat me down to explain the potential ramifications that could be caused by Amadi being out of school for three weeks. It appears that other parents would complain that there was a school space not being utilized. How would they know, I countered, as we are talking about three weeks, not three years? "Ahh, Chineme," remonstrated the Deputy Head, "it's all about bums on seats."

And there we had it – the school was concerned about "bums on seats." Never mind that my daughter had been at the school for five years and could not read or write. Never mind that it had taken over four years to arrive at the point where she was to be removed from the school for a period in order to remediate the failings of the system towards her learning. Never mind that she was due to be separated from her peers for some intensive reading instruction. And never mind that the trip away would mean the world to her in terms of character building and preparation for the changes to be made in the months ahead.

I made it absolutely clear that my main concern was Amadi's future; the fact that that appeared to conflict with their main concern of "bums on seats" was totally irrelevant to me. I was taking Amadi on the trip and they would just have to do whatever it was that they felt they had to do. I intimated that perhaps a court case brought against me by the very local education authority that had consistently denied Amadi the special education provision that she required, would be the perfect opportunity for their concerns and my concerns concerning Amadi's education to be properly aired.

A few days before we were due to leave for the trip I received a formal letter, by post, informing me that the request for Amadi's extended leave of absence had been reviewed and had been authorized.

CHAPTER THIRTEEN

Breaking through Barriers

Amadi and I proceeded to have a wonderful three weeks of travelling and growing together. The absolute highlight for Amadi was on the final day of the Canadian seminar. All of the participants were presented with a block of wood and invited to break through it as a symbol of breaking through their particular barriers. I made a feeble first attempt and inevitably failed as all that I was focusing on at the crucial moment was the possible damage to my right hand (again). I was however triumphant the second time around as I focused on pursuing Amadi's right to an appropriate education!

My protective instincts did not want Amadi to attempt breaking through her board – after all, she was merely nine (and with low muscle tone) whereby the other girls there ranged from 11 to 17. However, Amadi insisted on it but had an obviously painful first attempt which caused her to weep while clutching her hand to her chest. I cuddled her gently and told her she was not to attempt it again for fear of damaging her delicate limb.

Through her tears however, Amadi was adamant that she was going to do it. I could tell by the look on her face that there was simply nothing I could do to stop her, apart from removing her from the proceedings. On the basis that one of the objectives of our trip was to bolster her confidence and self-belief, it was extremely important that she was given every opportunity to attempt that which she very clearly wished to do. I therefore took a step back and prayed. Lo and behold, Amadi broke through the board! Every one of the participants had stopped what they were doing while Amadi had prepared herself mentally. She stood as she was told to do with her feet slightly apart. She was well balanced and focused on the task at hand.

Amadi's success brought screeches and howls of delight from everyone. She was hugged and kissed from all quarters with me leading the fray. The pride that she felt in herself at that moment was tangible. As was mine in the sheer persistence and determination of my little girl, despite the odds that the universe had given her when she was dealt her Williams Syndrome card. The barrier that Amadi had envisioned breaking through, as she mentally and physically prepared herself was the wall beyond which she would learn to read and write.

CHAPTER FOURTEEN

Early Life Changing Adjustments

We returned from our trip with a few days to spare before Amadi was to begin the new phase of her life at the learning centre. The time was used to get over the jet-lag and sheer exhaustion of the past three weeks of travelling, personal development and growth. Within my mountain of unopened mail was one from SENAS confirming Amadi's start date at the centre and the 10 week period there. Despite me being troubled about the emphasis on the period stated, I concentrated on what had been achieved and prepared for our new regime.

I had been left completely on my own to work out the logistics of Amadi's time at the learning centre. Amadi was not provided with any transportation or assistance either by the education authority or by social services, despite her disability. I pushed on regardless, since Amadi learning to read was an absolute priority. The sessions involved hourly intensives with alternating practitioners at the centre. Amadi would have a five minute break in between where I would chat with her about what she did and offer encouragement and refreshments. I was therefore committed to remaining at the centre while Amadi was there.

Inevitably, the fact that I had been left with no support in taking care of Amadi's journey to and from the centre, and in remaining there for her, had a devastating impact on my home business. I was unable to put in the hours required and consequently my income all but ceased. I recall this period as being a very frightening and emotionally turbulent one. I was self-employed. I was a single parent of a daughter with learn- ing difficulties with no other support. The agencies involved provided Amadi with no assistance for attending the learning centre (as they would have done had she attended at the special school where they wanted her to go despite her being able to learn nothing there). I therefore had to take care of Amadi's learning needs totally alone. My ability to continue my work was severely compromised. I endeavored to carry out relevant tasks in the early mornings and very late into the nights but, since the bulk of my work involved speaking to people on the telephone (network marketing), this could not be done at a decent hour. The learning centre was no place for me to try to conduct my business in the presence of the staff and other children there.

Amadi's hours at the centre were initially from two in the afternoon until six in the evening. This meant us being away from home from one until seven o'clock. They were very tiring days – for Amadi and me. The London traffic was always hor- rendous to navigate. By the end of the first week it was clear that the final hour was not very productive for Amadi due to tiredness and so a different schedule was agreed, to begin in her third week. Amadi would learn from 11am to one in the afternoon, have a break for lunch and then resume from two until four in the afternoon. These times worked much better for Amadi but of course meant us leaving home before ten in the morning and therefore there was even less time for me to try to earn some semblance of a living.

CHAPTER FIFTEEN

Lack of Support and Defensiveness

I received notification of a meeting for the Governing Body of Amadi's school to take place during Amadi's second week at the centre. Given that we were returning home very late in the evening, I clearly could not attend. Two days later, I received official notification of having been disqualified from continued membership of the Governing Body due to me not sending in my apology for non-attendance. This I greeted with good grace as there was no point in being a member if I could not attend. I did however consider it rather petty to state that no apology was sent when the SENCO knew perfectly well of my situation and had provided no form of support whatsoever.

A few days later I was included in an email notification sent out by the Head Teacher inviting all of the Governing Body to go out for a celebratory Christmas meal. I responded by alerting her to the fact that I was no longer a governor and provided her with my explanation for not sending in my apologies. I wanted her to know that I did take my responsibilities as a governor seriously and that it was merely circumstances that made it very difficult for me to attend on occasion. I went on to relay the good news that as early as Amadi's second week on the program she had achieved some positive results. Rather than merely sound out letters within words without being able to process the whole sound, Amadi was beginning to put letters and words together! I explained the system they were using at the centre and the fact that I was very excited at the relatively rapid developments.

To my utter dismay, the response I received, rather than being accepting (and why not congratulatory?) of Amadi's achievements, was entirely defensive in nature. I was told that it was not the SENCO's responsibility to make my apologies to the Governing Body as she was not a governor herself. I was told that it was not possible for the school to have provided the kind of learning that Amadi was now obtaining given the school's constraints. I was also told that the school was quite unaware of where Amadi was and what the details of her placement were as they had not had any contact from SENAS!

My response dealt only with the assertion that the school had no details of where Amadi was and I questioned whether it was beyond the wit of man for the SENCO and SENAS to communicate with each other? Since when was it my personal duty as a parent to keep each of those State designated agencies, i.e. the school and the education authority, in touch with one another? Is it not sufficient that I alone had pushed and pushed for an appropriate education for my daughter? That I alone did the research provided all of the information and made Amadi's placement a reality? That I had then been left to fend alone with the logistics of getting Amadi there and back? That I alone was monitoring and, indeed, was interested in her progress?

Progress achieved during her second week as compared with *none* in the preceding five years?

I thereafter received a response accusing me of accusing the school "as a whole" of doing "nothing for Amadi!" The petulant tone of the communication actually exhausted me. I reminded the Head Teacher that she was actually personally supportive of the placement and had made suggestions as to the length of Amadi's day and what she considered she could and could not manage. How then could it be said that she knew nothing of Amadi's placement? It was the school's duty, through its very own Special Educational Needs Co-coordinator, to liaise with the education authority's Special Educational Needs Assessment Service about the children over whom they have responsibility, especially those, like Amadi, whom have Statements of Special Education Need. It certainly was not rocket science. And it certainly was not yet another responsibility that this beleaguered parent was prepared to accept.

I did however provide them with the wording of Amadi's proposed new SEN as SENAS had provided it to me. I also suggested that the SENCO make some arrangements with the learning centre for her to attend to discuss with them Amadi's progress and the potential for assisting more of the school's children (rather than have me also facilitate these, as the Head Teacher had suggested).

CHAPTER SIXTEEN
Blatant Disingenuousness

Midway through Amadi's third week at the centre, she approached me absolutely beaming with joy — accompanied by her instructor; they both informed me of Amadi reading four sentences! Amadi had read four sentences! Wow, this really was the stuff of dreams. Amadi was discovering the magic of learning at last. In just three weeks, Amadi had begun to understand how to read after more than five years in the literacy wilderness. My daughter, who had literally been abandoned by the system that was supposed to provide her with "an appropriate education," was indeed becoming a reader, despite, not because of, the state system.

Bolstered by these phenomenal developments, I wrote to SENAS requesting that they continue the placement, at least in accordance with the centre's further assessment and recommendations when these were made. I received a terse response that agreement had only been provided for the initial 10 week period and that they would not agree to anything further. I wrote to them again to remind them that they had based their initial agreement to the placement on the "further informa-tion" that they had received from the Williams Syndrome Foundation (which detailed the kind of learning that would be beneficial) and the report of the diagnostic assessment carried out by the learning centre. That report recommended an *initial* period of 10 to 12 weeks to develop Amadi's concept imagery skills and then *further* periods in order to work on developing her reading and math skills.

I reported on the progress that Amadi had made in such a short period, which provided conclusive proof that the learning methods employed were astoundingly effective for Amadi. I questioned how this can then be curtailed when it would mean that her initial period here would have been entirely in vain? How could that make any sense at all? Now that the ground-work had been laid, Amadi should continue at the centre for at least two hours per day and then attend her school in the afternoons.

I was informed that the matter would need to be discussed by their senior management team before a definitive response could be provided (despite the earlier blanket refusal). So then I waited. And I waited.

Meanwhile, the school SENCO had finally contacted the centre and made an appointment to attend to observe Amadi during one of her classes, and to meet with the centre Director for an overview of the process and Amadi's progress. The meet-ing was scheduled for the end of Amadi's fifth week there and the SENCO duly attended along with one of Amadi's learning support assistants from the school.

We all observed Amadi in a session for some time before moving on to meet with the Director. There then followed a bizarre two hour period wherein the SENCO asserted that similar, if not the same, processes were used at the school! Rather than challenge her on this rather outlandish notion,

I enquired why, then, were these processes not available for Amadi? Her answer was that it was only the designated children within the school's Speech and Language Unit who could benefit from them. What of the other children in the school who could not read, I asked? They apparently were not entitled to it – only those referred to them under a certain system could access it. Apparently, the school's metaphorical hands were tied when it came to all the others who could not properly read. I felt so embarrassed for this SENCO who appeared to speak with much resignation when relaying such bewildering news.

Amadi's learning support assistant asserted that she had tried in vain to teach Amadi words and phrases which she would then forget in their entirety by the following day. I reassured her that that was due solely to the strategies adopted by the school system. Amadi required the sensory-cognitive process of learning for it to be effective as had been so graphically demonstrated at the centre, and that would necessitate the adoption of those processes for them to be administered effectively in the school.

The Director informed them that they would be provided with processes that they could use to ensure that Amadi's learning continued at school. The SENCO stated that it was impossible for the processes to be incorporated into the school as Amadi is just one of 30 in her class. I suggested that the processes could be used for Amadi and all of the other failing children in a place away from the other pupils. Again, the SENCO stated that this would be impossible because there was absolutely no room, no area, and no space where this could be achieved. The school could not under any circumstances physically incorporate the processes. The attitude portrayed was defeatist in the extreme. There was certainly no will to facilitate any kind of change in order to bring some semblance of learning to those children who were so dismissively left to fail within the school which, of course, included Amadi. These assertions were of course in direct contradiction to what the SENCO had previously asserted concerning the school's continuing use of such processes.

CHAPTER SEVENTEEN

Containment Versus Advancement

The status quo, it seemed, had to be preserved at all costs. So what of progress? Why such a rigid resistance to change in an environment where all children were meant to benefit from learning?

These remain my abiding questions, questions that ought to resonate throughout the state education sector where children are being systematically failed by a system designed to provide each one of them with an appropriate education. I had not come across one person within the system that was prepared to make a stand and work for change. Every single administrator with which I had come into contact was intent on maintaining the status quo. That was why I was seen by them as a thorn in their side. As someone who was intent on upsetting their apple cart. As someone who expected them to do things differently to the way they had always done. As someone who actually expected her daughter, whom after all had learning difficulties, to actually learn to read!

In one of my many written communications to SENAS I asked them why they were not willing to take the initiative and do something brilliant instead of merely rolling out the status quo. Their status quo which, I contended and still maintain is actually contrary to the true letter of the law. They have policies and procedures which, although inefficient for a very high number of children with learning difficulties, they churn out anyway, irrespective of their ineffectuality and with scant regard for these children who are herded through the system and come out the other side as illiterate as when they went in. How can any self- respecting educator or educational administrator be satisfied with such a state of affairs? It beggars belief that, in the twenty-first century, children are being dealt with in this way, literally because of their disabilities? This has to be, to my mind, the worst form of disability discrimination – inadequate or unfair treatment *purely* on the basis of a disability – and there are also laws in place against that.

I had introduced to the school and the local education authority a way of teaching that could change the course of many children's lives by simply being able to teach them how to read in a way that the children understand. Surely, reading, writing and comprehension are the basic tenets of any kind of education, let alone the espoused notion of an "appropriate" education? Instead of at least looking into this different approach, it is dismissed out of hand as being something that they "simply do not do." Why not? Why do they simply not do this? Why do they simply not allow for the alternative method of teaching that would give so many children access to the magic of learning?

The common mantra I have come to hear is that anything out of their usual rituals would be "an inefficient use of public resources." Ha! I wish they would not insult our intelligence. Or am I being too generous in suggesting that they must know that this position is absolute balderdash and can easily be proved not to be the case at all? Have they computed the huge cost to society of *NOT* teaching these children to read and write? Have they computed the huge cost of these children growing to be totally, or even partially, *dependent* on the State during their adult years? And this would simply be because they are not given basic *access* to the school curriculum and, indeed, all that life in general has to offer.

Even if the matter were to be considered in micro rather than macro terms – have they computed the huge costs of placing children with similar learning issues as Amadi in their heavily funded 'special schools' as compared with a highly effective process-based model such as that to which Amadi has gained access, albeit briefly (so far)? I mean the huge cost of placing children with learning difficulties out of sight, and consequently, out of mind, in these 'special schools' where they will still leave the system unable to read and write? Of course, after that they are then to be herded into their next adult 'special placement' to the additional, astronomical cost to the state?

Something has got to be done about this broken and inadequate system that is not catering for a great many of our children with special learning needs and disabilities. Something has just got to be done. I consider this to be an intolerable state of affairs. I have fought hard for my particular child and I will continue to raise awareness of these injustices within our mainstream state education system. This is a system where the strategies and policies are not about learning and advancement generally, but are merely about containment of a growing minority.

CHAPTER EIGHTEEN

Reading, Achieving and Believing

Meanwhile, back at the learning centre, Amadi continued to exceed all expectations. On the drive to the centre at the beginning of her sixth week, we played a game of her reading whatever she could from the sides of vehicles and the signs on the shop doorways. She managed the one syllable words without too much difficulty and the longer ones with some encouragement. Two examples of her successes that day will always stick in my mind: "Loot.com" and "Red Planet." To verify the latter, I pulled over to have a look at what she was reading. To my absolute delight, there was indeed a restaurant right there, called "Red Planet!" I must have been the proudest parent in the entire world at that moment, hearing my cognitively challenged princess actually **reading** words previously unknown to her like an absolute trooper!

Instances like this made the whole grueling business worthwhile. Many have asked me how I managed to continue fighting the good fight against all the odds. It may appear martyr-like to believe so passionately about an issue that one gets so totally subsumed within it to the apparent detriment of all else. However, so far as my own daughter is concerned, I do not believe that there is any alternative. I am her mother. I brought her into the world. There is no other single person who could, or would, advocate on her behalf in this way. It is all-consuming. In order to properly access the world in general – let alone the school curriculum – Amadi needs to be able to read. There are processes that specialize in teaching her and others with similar difficulties the *process* of learning **how** to read. Why is there such blatant resistance within the state system to these people gaining access to these well-documented processes?

The authorities have demonstrated all too clearly that they have no desire for Amadi and others like her to learn to read. They do not see it as their responsibility, and continue to state that it is not cost effective for them to ensure that cognitively challenged children be taught to read, irrespective of the availability of the processes so to do. I have been told on numerous occasions that it would not be "an efficient use of public funds" for Amadi to be taught how to read. This is despite the mammoth costs of having her within a system that chooses *not* **to** teach her to read.

It makes no sense to me whatsoever. It will be interesting indeed to hear the judgment of a court of law on this issue – I cannot see that any learned person could rule that a whole raft of society must be left uneducated in favor of relatively small cost savings in the very short term. Time will certainly tell since, as of Amadi's seventh week at the learning centre, I am yet to hear from SENAS as to whether or not she will be allowed to continue her newly discovered process of learning.

It appears that they may actually deem it more cost effective to negate the cost of the ten week initial stage of her learning just so that Amadi may return to the State system and continue on her journey to abject failure. Should this be their decision, I will of course have no option but to turn to the law – five years of trying to persuade them that Amadi and children like her are indeed part of their responsibility for the provision of an appropriate education would have failed, and there is not a lot more that my single voice can do alone.

I have met with my Member of Parliament who also wrote to the Children's Minister – to no avail. I have contacted the Director of MENCAP who put me in touch with their education policy person – to no avail. It was a concern to me that they advocate inclusion but told me that they do not focus on the *process* of learning in the way that I described. Thus, it appeared that to the judiciary was all that was left for me to turn in order for them to interpret and enforce the legislation that I believe is all too clear, but is being ignored in far too many instances – my own daughter's case included.

There are days, especially when Amadi appears not to be co-operating with her instructors, that I despair about having to keep on fighting like I've had to do. Amadi at times gets frustrated; it is ironic that as she comprehends more, she expects so much more from herself! I then wonder whether I should just let her be and stop torturing myself with the inadequacies of this education system. Amadi misses her friends at school – should I just let her play and forget about her learning to read? No, no, no! I snap out of such self-questioning thoughts pretty sharpish when I project into the future and try to imagine what Amadi's life will be like trying to navigate the world without me, and not being able to read.

I shudder in disgust at a system that can, and does, so easily make that the norm for far too many people. These thoughts then re-energize me in continuing in my battles to persuade the powers that be to confront this issue – an issue that remains hidden from far too many people whom are not aware of this educational underworld where the basic act of learning to read is actively, and quite purposefully, withheld for far too many children.

CHAPTER NINETEEN

From Desolation to Desperation

On the last day of Amadi's seventh week at the centre I received an email from SENAS confirming that they would no longer fund Amadi's learning. I had requested that she be allowed to continue at the centre for just two hours a day to build on what had already been achieved to ensure her learning to read was continued. They had flatly refused this on the same grounds as before – that they did not consider it an efficient use of resources to provide Amadi with an education that was appropriate for her particular needs. To add insult to injury, they then stated that they would again "consult" with Amadi's school and the 'special school' that was mentioned some time ago (which was shown not to be able to provide Amadi with an appropriate education). It will be recalled that this school actually had a young girl with Williams Syndrome attend their environs for over five years. She left there not being able to read.

My emotions at that point are very difficult to explain. I had not really expected anything better of this local education authority's special educational needs and assessment service, but given Amadi's progress and the enormous amount of correspondence, reports and evidence with which they had been provided over the years, would it not have been possible for them to actually do some research to see whether they could find an establishment that *could* provide my daughter with an appropriate education? I had found one and had given them the information. They had allowed her to begin her initial learning there in accordance with the diagnostic evaluation, but then decided to pull the rug from under her feet to send her back to a place where she can continue to fail as before.

I felt frustrated. I felt extremely let down. I felt terribly alone. I felt exasperated. That morning I looked at my little angel who had only just discovered the magic of learning and tears welled up in my eyes. I quickly dropped Amadi off at the learning centre and then completely broke down in my car. I sobbed, and sobbed, and sobbed as if just the act of me physically vibrating would somehow shake away the injustice of it all. I eventually stopped sobbing and looked into the distance through my car window. I saw a lady with some young children in red and grey uniforms as they skipped happily down the street. I imagined that they must be on their way to school. I wondered if her children had ever had an issue with their reading. I wondered how it must feel to just be able to take your child to school and not have to worry about whether they will ever be taught how to read and write? I thought again about the law – my child, as well as those happy children down the road, is entitled to an appropriate education. I imagined that those children were getting an education appropriate to their needs. Why was it that my child was being denied an education appropriate to her needs?

The law states that the appropriate provision could be sought in a school *or other* institution or indeed, abroad! Why is it then that this SENAS deems it an *in*efficient use of their resources to fund a placement at this learning centre, for just two hours a day for a defined period, to ensure the appropriate educational provision for my daughter? Indeed, to ensure that she learns the most fundamental tenet of *any* education, i.e. how to read? My daughter is the only child in her school with her particular condition and SENAS informs me that there are only four children with WS in the entire borough. It is clear that SENAS have not made the same type of provision before. I was at a loss as to where next to turn. I was on the brink of bankruptcy, not being able to run my home business effectively for some time. I knew that the matter would need to go before the courts and that would entail a further financial burden. I needed to do something more immediate – Amadi had just a couple more weeks left at the centre before the local education authority pulled the plug. I turned my considerations to the national press.

CHAPTER TWENTY

A Glimmer of Hope

I recalled reading a newspaper column of a journalist whom had a daughter with Down's syndrome. From my recollection, his daughter did not have any difficulties with reading but I hoped that he would have some empathy with my position as a parent with a daughter who had a congenital abnormality. I proceeded to write to him, detailing Amadi's and my situation, in the hope that he would agree to write about what we were going through. I prayed that such an article would raise awareness of the problems we and countless other families faced. I also hoped that such widespread press coverage would uncover details of education lawyers with experience of the issues over which we would undoubtedly very shortly need to litigate.

I sent the letter by email very early on a Saturday morning after yet another sleepless night and hoped that he might check his work emails over the weekend. Having heard nothing by the Monday I assumed that he had not checked his inbox and would surely respond within the next couple of days. Meanwhile, I toyed with the idea of sending out a general press release and see which, if any, of the national and local press would be interested enough to pick up the story. Then I had a period of reflection. I had been so knocked back by SENAS's decision to pull the plug on Amadi's learning that I think I must have slipped into panic mode. I was exhausted through worry and lack of sleep and, without the funds to take direct and immediate legal action against the education authority's decision; I felt I needed to get the word out somehow – in any way.

I discussed our situation with other parents at the learning centre and they provided details of other journalists with an education brief with whom I could get into contact. We also toyed with the possibility of me meeting with SENAS once again, along with the learning centre Director so that they could benefit from a more in-depth understanding of how and what Amadi was being taught there. It was agreed that it was worth a shot, although I remained skeptical.

As soon as we returned home that evening I wrote to my contact at SENAS requesting such a meeting. I had asked that they refrain from pulling the plug just yet so that a more realistic cost/benefit review could be undertaken with staff from the centre whom had met with Amadi prior to starting the program, could comment on the progress she had made and provide an experienced projection of how much longer would be realistic for Amadi to continue before she could be said to be able to read at a level where she would be able to access, on at least a basic level, what her classmates were being taught in school.

I emphasized that stopping the program and sending Amadi back to school would be a thoroughly fruitless exercise – she had made progress but did not yet know enough to be able to grasp any reading matter being discussed in the classroom. It would in effect have been a total waste of everyone's time and resources for the past couple of months. Not to mention the effect on Amadi – now and into the future. I also stated that we had a legitimate expectation that they would at least follow the recommendations as set out in the initial diagnostic report – the report which they stated gave rise to them changing their minds about Amadi attending the centre in the first place. I pondered whether they could use the opportunity to consider sending some of the borough's teachers to be trained in the learning processes at the centre, so that they could then take that knowledge back and utilize it *within* the schools to benefit so many other children who required such processes in order to just be able to learn.

I emailed the letter and waited. I also decided to copy the letter to the Director of Education to ensure that there could be no misunderstanding at all about what I was requesting , i.e. at least a chance to explain further the processes involved in the program (should the matter ultimately end up in the press or, indeed, in the courts).

Later that afternoon I received their response. To my relief, they had agreed to the meeting! They had provided a list of alternative dates as I had requested and I immediately passed these on to the centre for their director to choose one that was convenient for her, and then sent back my confirmation of the agreed meeting date and time.

CHAPTER TWENTY-ONE

To Support, or Not to Support?

The next day I was chatting with a lady whom I had presumed was the mother of one of the centre's attendees. She explained that she was not in fact the girl's mother but was her *school one-to-one learning support assistant*! I enquired as to how she came to be accompanying the young girl and was informed that their London local education authority's SENAS was funding her attendance at the centre and, as the young girl's school support, she was deemed the best one to accompany her to the centre. I thought, what a difference a district makes!

On further enquiry however, it appears that their authority's SENAS was also initially against the idea of the pupil attending the learning centre but her school Head teacher, Deputy Head and their SENCO supported the placement fully and even attended the meetings with their SENAS to argue for the pupil's attendance there. The support assistant told of how the school video recorded the meeting so that there was a permanent record of what was said and done. Wow!

How refreshing to know that there are schools out there who do understand the importance of the cognitive-sensory function in the process of learning, and are actually willing to stand up against their education authorities in full support of individual pupils. I consider that such support would be invaluable for the parents whom often have to go through the grueling processes alone, against the might of their district councils.

It must be said that Amadi's Head teacher initially provided me with support privately; but to have the school also put their considerable weight directly behind the requests to SENAS would have been a fantastic addition to my parental pleadings. Encouraged by the slightest possibility that Amadi's school may also agree to attend the scheduled meeting along with the learning centre, I thought it couldn't hurt to ask them. However, that day happened to be the last day of the school term before the Christmas break and so I had to wait for over two weeks before I could get a definitive answer to messages that I had left on the SENCO's voicemail, plus emails that I had sent to her and the Head teacher.

And so I waited, and waited. I knew that in the past the Head teacher had read and responded to email out of school hours, but given that it was the Christmas and New Year break, she may have been away or simply taking a well- deserved rest from the day job. For me however, it was the longest two and a half weeks because I felt as though I was in limbo. I began to fear that I no longer had the support of the school and, even worse, Amadi may no longer have a place there. The Head teacher had previously assured me that Amadi would have her place at the school for as long as we wanted it, but I imagined that perhaps they were now fed up with Amadi's non-attendance and my continued pleas for their support in the quest for Amadi's learning. I grew increasingly paranoid about what the reasons for this non-communication could be. I was used to having the SENCO not respond to my communications, but the Head teacher would normally respond as soon as she was able.

I imagine that these kinds of emotional turmoil and near paranoia are probably quite common for parents going through similar issues to my own. It is a state of being that I would wager that other 'ordinary' families could *never* imagine experiencing. It is a state of being that I never imagined I would be experiencing when I gave birth to my beautiful, precious daughter, especially in a country where there is compulsory state education and a welfare system which is meant to also cater for those outside of the norm. But here I was, totally alone in my thoughts, considerations and deliberations. My daughter was to have her new-found magic of learning snatched away from her. She was to return to the system that had totally failed her so that it could continue to fail her. And there was absolutely nothing that I could do for her – for the time being.

CHAPTER TWENTY-TWO

Communications and Distractions

I was encouraged when, a few days after Christmas, I received an email from the wife of the journalist that I had written to a couple of weeks before. He had indeed read my email and passed it on to his wife who is also a well-known journalist. She had some involvement with a children's charity in London and she advised me to contact them for support and to mention her name in the process. I did contact the charity but they were confined to a different area of London and so could not be of any assistance to me. But the mere fact that someone else had taken an interest in our situation, however slight or fleeting, meant the world to me. Perhaps I was not alone after all. I continued to wait for a response from the school, but with a much lighter state of mind than before I received the very kind communication from the journalists.

There was of course no end of term break for Amadi who continued her attendance at the learning centre, except for the

Public holidays. Her abilities continued to improve albeit slowly – but at least we were headed in the right direction, rather than regressing, as she had been doing without the cognitive-sensory process of learning with which she was now being provided. I wept silently every time I allowed myself to contemplate what it would mean for her should the program be stopped – both educationally, and emotionally. There were just two weeks remaining of the initial foundation period. It was in the lap of the Universe as to what would happen after that.

When the school resumed, I continued to wait anxiously for a response from the education authority. The abject loneliness and stark realization of the mammoth obstacles that lay ahead loomed over me like a thick, dark cloud. Not to mention the massive debts that I had now racked up in a desperate bid to keep our heads above water. Our everyday living expenses were meager but when added to the house payments, the bills, taxes and everything else, things were looking very grim indeed. It was at that time that my car's battery then decided to die on me after almost six years of loyal service! The mechanic informed me that I was very lucky indeed to get more than three years out of it. But why now, I wondered? My brother came to my aid and ensured that a new battery was fitted – our daily trips to the learning centre demanded it.

That night I worked well into the early hours on my internet marketing business and noticed that the SENCO had responded by email to my communications some hours earlier. With trepidation, I opened and read the message. With a sigh of relief, I noted that we had not yet been ex-communicated in that she stated, "it would be useful" for her to attend the meeting at the local education authority. I presumed that this must mean that Amadi still had her place at the school – the last thing we needed right now was to have to start looking for another state school when the teaching methods would be no different to where she was currently registered (and indeed where she had always been and where her friends attended).

The next morning, I sent an email thanking the SENCO and, as we got ready to leave for the learning centre, one of my outside pipes began to spray volumous amounts of water all over the side of the house and into our next door neighbor's garden. On further examination, it appeared to me that we must have sustained a burst pipe. It had been bitterly cold of late with minus zero temperatures. It seemed that when something starts to go wrong, absolutely everything goes wrong! With no money and absolutely no plumbing skills whatsoever, I left for the learning centre pondering what the Universe had in store for us next, and whether the house would still be standing when we returned home later that evening!

As luck would have it, our house was indeed still standing when we returned home, and I called in a plumber to investigate the problem. It appears that the pipe had not burst but had just come apart at some juncture. With some fiddling around and stopping something off, the problem was contained and my mind could once again return to my daughter's education.

CHAPTER TWENTY-THREE
Brickbats and Stalemate

As Amadi's word attack skills developed, we had started to play word games whereby I would ask her to spell random words without prior warning. She was able to make some remarkable self-corrections and phonetically spell even the long and unfamiliar words. Her visualization skills had improved so very much in such a short time! Surely, I mused, SENAS would not pull the plug on her learning at the centre once the centre Director reported on Amadi's progress? Only time would tell.

I had a final review meeting at the centre during Amadi's penultimate week (and the week before the meeting with SENAS). Amadi's final assessment showed that in some areas she had gained almost two chronological years with her comprehension and word attack skills! This is amazing stuff. In less than ten weeks, Amadi's capabilities had made such a significant improvement – improvements that just would not have been made had she not attended at the centre; improvements that children with similar cognitive difficulties just do not make within the state sector. Where's the justice? Despite legislation purporting to ensure an appropriate education for **all** of the country's children, a significant number do not discover the magic of reading simply because they are not taught in an **appropriate** way for their particular learning needs.

I had also noticed that Amadi's reasoning skills had improved dramatically on a day-to-day level. The centre Director explained that this is normally associated with the use of neurons in the brain that previously had not been extensively exercised. By using the sensory-language connection to learning, Amadi's **cognition** was actually being improved. There was still a long way to go before Amadi could be said to be a true reader but, step by step, she was progressing well.

Amadi's initial block of sessions at the centre was due to conclude during the second week of January – the week in which the meeting with SENAS was to take place on the Monday. I therefore agreed a day plan for Amadi whereby she would spend three mornings at the centre and the rest of the time back at her primary school. I emailed the details to the school SENCO so that they were aware of Amadi's imminent return but I received no response. On the Monday morning therefore, we set off for school not knowing what kind of reception awaited us. Amadi had not attended the school for over three months and so it was a strange feeling re-entering that environment.

The first person we met was the Head teacher who informed us that the SENCO was expecting us. With a sigh of relief I proceeded to her office. She informed me that she had received my emails confirming the time of the meeting with SENAS later that morning, and the details concerning Amadi's return to school. There was no explanation as to why I had not had any response to those emails, and I did not pursue that. We spoke briefly about the meeting and agreed to meet at the SENAS offices at the appointed time.

My contact at SENAS was the only representative at the meeting. She explained that rather than have any other senior management team members attend, she would report back to them prior to reaching a decision about whether or not they would agree to funding further sessions for Amadi at the centre. Despite this assurance, I got the distinct feeling throughout the 90 minute meeting that the decision had already been made, as she constantly stated that they considered any further funding to be an *inefficient* use of their resources…

The centre Director gave a brief presentation about the processes used to teach at the centre and the progress that Amadi had made. She explained that Amadi was at a fragile stage of her learning and recommended that she would require a further block of 12 to 15 weeks of intensive instruction for three hours per day in order to solidify her reading ability.

The SENCO stressed that the school understood the importance of the learning centre to Amadi's reading improvement, but explained that the school did not have the staff with appropriate training, nor did they have the right environment for the processes to be effectively implemented within the school. She made various suggestions as to how the situation could be improved, such as SENAS procuring places at the centre's workshops for the benefit of Amadi's support assistants, or allowing Amadi to have the benefit of the school's Speech and Language Unit (SLU) which had strict criteria for admission. The criteria were that the children had to have speech and language difficulties but no cognitive impairments. Apparently, the SLU utilized similar methods of teaching to the learning centre but it was only the children *within the unit* who could benefit from this (despite there being many children within the school whom ideally should have had access to the processes purportedly used).

SENAS made it clear that any training of the school staff would need to be met out of the school's own budget. It was also made clear that Amadi would not qualify for the school's SLU on the basis that her speech and language were not her primary difficulty; plus, her cognition was not of a high enough level for her to qualify! Thus, yet again, Amadi and countless others seemingly fell between the cracks – not benefiting from the mainstream system, nor the specialized system said to exist within the state sector.

SENAS continually pushed the issue of Amadi attending the special school that they had previously identified, again on the basis of cost and the smaller class sizes. I again explained that Amadi would not benefit there – it would merely be a matter of convenient containment rather than somewhere that could teach her in the way that she needed to be taught in order for her to be able to learn. The same old issues were bandied back and forth and the SENAS representative frequently made references to what they would need to demonstrate at the Special Educational Needs and Disability Tribunal. This is the appeal body where disputes had usually to go prior to instituting proceedings in the law courts. I reminded her that they had agreed to Amadi embarking on the sessions at the centre on the basis of the initial diagnostic report and recommendations. What they now wanted to do was to pull the rug out from under her at a crucial stage and not in accordance with the recommendations initially made – how can that be justified? Amadi was learning to read; did that not count for anything, I asked? The response from Brent Council's Special Educational Needs and Assessment service was, "reading is not a necessity – she can do other things." I, not for the first time, was stunned into silence.

Later that afternoon I received a message and email from SENAS informing me, as previously indicated, that they would no longer be funding the sessions at the learning centre and that they were going to 'consult' with Amadi's school as well as the special school to see which could offer her a place. They stated that Amadi could continue only until the end of January and then that would be it. Although this was expected, it still felt like a stab through the heart. Despite hearing from the centre Director about Amadi's progress, and the school SENCO about the inability of the state sector to administer appropriate processes for teaching children in a similar situation to Amadi, SENAS would not be moved. I sat very still for a very long time contemplating the further battles that lay ahead – it was clear to me that, since the **Head** of SENAS believed that "reading is not a necessity – (Amadi) can do other things" I had clearly been wasting my time. It was made abundantly clear that legal due process was the only avenue left open to us.

CHAPTER TWENTY-FOUR

Domestic Economics and Academics

I was due to meet with my accountant that very afternoon and so my attention had to turn once more to my dire financial situation. Things were extremely critical. Unless more income was forthcoming, repossession of our home was inevitable. I already had other creditors constantly writing to me and telephoning me about their missed payments or outstanding balances. I felt as though my head was spinning. Yet I had to keep on top of it all. I had to ensure that I kept on top of our financial situation. I worked very late into the night, every night, to try to hold that aspect together. And now I also had to focus on appealing against the local authority's decision to stop funding my daughter's appropriate education.

The SENAS representative had stated that they are "not obliged to provide the *best* education." I asked her how a process to teach children the very fundamental skill of reading can be said to be called the "best" education when clearly it was the only one available for Amadi's learning to read? The state sector did not provide Amadi with the teaching she needed to be able to read. The learning centre did. No doubt there must be other paying establishments here and abroad that not only catered for reading and math, but also a much wider spectrum of learning for our children with learning disabilities. How can a centre focusing on comprehension, reading and math be described as the "best" education in a way that then discounts them from teaching my child to read where the state sector had abjectly failed?

At the meeting with SENAS, it was starkly evident that no real thought had gone into what it was that Amadi required. Although they were adamant that she could not continue at the learning centre, they were still stating that they would be consulting with Amadi's school and the special school previously mentioned as possible contenders for the rest of her primary schooling. It all depended on which school was prepared to have her. There was no concern as to **how** either school could teach her to read. The final statement of educational needs would state one or the other school. End of discussion.

I later met with the SENCO prior to collecting Amadi from school. We discussed the meeting with SENAS and, although she stated that the school was happy for Amadi to continue attending, she also stressed once more that there was *nothing more* that they could offer Amadi. She then showed me details of an 'independent special school' in South-West London which catered for children with special needs from the ages of seven to 19. She said that Amadi could therefore go there now and not have to change schools again until her majority. I reminded her that we were talking about what would be a 20 mile round trip! She countered that a bus would be provided for the journey. Clearly, she had thought this one through. For someone stating that they were happy for Amadi to continue at the school, she was very eager to suggest alternatives. She also stated that next year in Year 6, the children were facing exams and intimated that it would be an exceptionally difficult time for Amadi (as though that was something new). It was quite incredible to me that, having failed to teach Amadi to read, the school system then expected her to take examinations! How farcical. I believe that this was the only reason that they wanted Amadi to go to a special school – so that she would not mess up their statistics when it came to the national school league tables.

Given her blatant attempt to have me remove Amadi from the only school that she had ever known, I asked the SENCO this straightforward question, "In your honest opinion, if resources, space, processes etc. were not in issue, do you really think that Amadi should be attending a special school?" She hesitated for a while and then said, "Well Chineme, I have a foot in both camps." Given this thoroughly unhelpful answer, I stuck to my belief that it would be emotionally damaging to Amadi to remove her from the school which she loved attending and from the only friends that she had ever known, to a totally alien environment at this late stage in her primary education. I reminded the SENCO that there was just a year to go and then Amadi would be moving to a secondary school. I had absolutely no intention of uprooting her now to a place where she **still** would not be taught to read. Sure enough, when I collected Amadi after her first day at school for several months, she was absolutely bursting with happiness and joy at being back in her school and interacting with all of her friends. I believe that SENAS and the SENCO see Amadi as merely a statistic – one that has to be dealt with by merely putting her away – out of **their** way, so that they can continue in their day jobs without any more hassle and strife about her needs, or my insistence on her receiving an education **appropriate** to her particular needs. This mother was certainly not going to be a willing participant or accomplice to their despicable objectives.

It was clear to me that, despite the SENCO attending the meeting with SENAS, I was very much alone in my endeavors. The Head Teacher had previously assured me that there would always be a place for Amadi in the school. And yet the SENCO was suggesting the contrary. I recalled that the Head Teacher had said nothing at all to me after referring me to the SENCO on Amadi's first day back at school. The tide had definitely turned. I felt that something very unpleasant was brewing, although I could not say what. All I could do was wait to receive Amadi's finalized statement and then be prepared to start the appeal process at all costs. Neither agency would have my consent for removing Amadi from her current placement. Half a day at the learning centre and half a day at school worked well for other children attending the learning centre. I would press on in my endeavors to continue this arrangement for Amadi or, of course, to get it re-instated after it was withdrawn.

During our meeting, the SENCO had assured me that we could go through the school's response to Amadi's Statutory Statement of Special Educational Needs together when it arrived. That at least should ensure that we were singing from the same hymn sheet so far as the education authority was concerned…

CHAPTER TWENTY-FIVE

Children in Statutory Need, Indeed

Amadi had just two weeks remaining at the learning centre in the mornings and her school in the afternoons. I still had to accompany her as, SENAS had insisted, it was not possible for Amadi to have transport in the middle of the day. This aspect of this whole sorry business would also feature in my appeal to the Tribunal and/or the courts, since, given Amadi's disability, I learned that transport **should indeed have been provided**. Many other attendees at the learning centre had been escorted there and back by their local education authorities, as part of their special educational needs.

Later that weekend, I received a letter from the Social Services department informing me that an earlier plea to them from me had been considered and, as a 'child in need,' Amadi had been allocated a social worker! At last, I thought, an agency within the system that can now also assist me in ensuring that Amadi receives what she is actually entitled to. I considered this development significant because, so far as children are concerned, this department's legal duty was to act in the ***best interests of the child***. I would however have to wait a couple of weeks more before meeting the allocated social worker, as she was said to currently be on annual leave. Oh well.

The following Monday morning, I met up with the learning support assistant of one of the other children at the learning centre whose local education authority **was** funding her placement there. She informed me that after the initial 12 weeks, ***another 12 weeks had now been approved*** for her. She was very sympathetic to Amadi's plight given that our funding had been pulled. We had a long discussion about the needs of her charge and those of Amadi. It was clear that the only reason that Amadi had got here in the first place was because of my advocating so strongly for her. I learned that the other girl's journey, although much shorter (a year, rather than four) was instigated by the ***school itself***. This gem of a learning support assistant had made it known that the girl she was supporting needed more than just what the school could provide. Their SENCO agreed and they both approached the girl's mother who also agreed that something more was required. They found out about the learning centre, lobbied their SENAS for it, and, as the child was found to be ***"in need,"*** the rest of her story was history.

I was encouraged not to give up and to continue advocating for Amadi. It was such a shame that Amadi's school were not of the same mindset as that other state mainstream school. That school went to great lengths to ensure that their children with special educational needs were taught appropriately. I was informed that the district in which that school was based had a very high incidence of children with special educational needs. The schools ensured that those children were pulled out of certain classes and put into others that proved more conducive to their learning needs. This particular girl was in Year 3, yet if there was an appropriate lesson going on in Reception, Year 1 or 2, the girl would have access to it. There were no brick walls as far as her learning was concerned. That school ensured that they took their responsibilities very seriously indeed – they themselves went all out to ensure that their pupils received an education appropriate for their pupils' individual needs. That was in stark contrast to Amadi's school which was adamant that *nothing* could be done for Amadi. Indeed, the 'rules' dictated that Amadi could not even benefit from the processes which were said to pertain *within the School's own* Speech and Language Unit, or even from being pulled out of classes for certain activities, due, they insisted, to a lack of physical space within the environs of the vast school grounds.

This situation further emphasizes the injustices within the state system. Bear in mind that there are many at the learning centre who had their places funded by their own families – those whom have the resources simply do it by themselves. It is those, like Amadi and the vast majority of children in society, whose parents simply cannot afford to pay outside of the mainstream system – for which they have already paid heavily through their income taxes and national insurance payments – whom get left out in the cold. The perpetuation of this two-tier system is then justified by districts such as ours that state that it is an ***inefficient use of their resources*** to teach children with learning difficulties simply to read. But clearly, there are other districts that deem it to be exactly what it should be, i.e. a very **efficient** use of their resources to ensure that their inhabitants are at least literate. Thus, there is also a two-tier system *within* the state sector – those districts that understand the **importance** of teaching their children to read, and those that simply do not.

CHAPTER TWENTY-SIX

Exclusion within Inclusion

As though my daily tribulations concerning Amadi's reading and her school situation was not enough, I learned of another matter that militated against my daughter. A friend of mine who has a daughter in the same class as Amadi asked me whether Amadi would be attending a week away that the school was arranging for her year group. This came as a complete surprise to me since, despite my communications with the school and the SENCO, not one word had been spoken to me about it. I had received no letters about it nor had Amadi been told or given any information about it. Amadi had been totally ignored. I felt, once again, as though I had been stabbed through the heart. It appeared that the school had not deemed it necessary to include Amadi in their considerations concerning the trip. She may as well have been invisible.

Many issues raced through my mind. It settled on a possible explanation that Amadi was not deemed fit for inclusion due to her disability of having Williams Syndrome. Not fit, due to her learning disability. We are talking of nine and ten year old children whom would require close supervision in any event; could it be that they considered Amadi would be too much like hard work for them – even with her one to one support? Or had Amadi already been cast out from their school in their own minds? I was never consulted and so had absolutely no idea what the reasons were. All I knew was that my consent was not sought, and no information had been provided; Amadi again had been treated as an absolute **non-person**. They did not even have the decency to approach me to advise me that Amadi could not go, with the reasons of why not, if that was the case. As in the situation with the talent competition a year prior, my daughter had again been discriminated against and the only reason that I can imagine for this is due to her particular disability. This was disability discrimination; absolutely unlawful within the mainstream school context – totally unfeasible within the concept of inclusion.

Amadi happened to be present when my friend mentioned the trip and she pleaded with me to let her go. As the tears welled up in my eyes, I explained that perhaps they already had their quota and that there were no more places available. I'm really not sure what went through her little mind at that precise moment, but she took my hand and proclaimed, "I want to stay with you, Mummy." Was there a realization for her of what had transpired and the reasons for it? Did she think I would be losing out if she were to go on the trip? Did she in that split second realize my inner pain and wanted to show that it was ok? Or did she really consider the implications and rationally decide that the trip was not for her? I really cannot say, and decided it was best not to discuss it further with her until I had a fuller understanding of the school's position. All I knew was that my little girl switched from near-tearful pleas to allow her to go, to a staunch resolution that she would not go. The matter was never raised by her to me again.

I thought about this situation again and again during the following days, and a week later I decided to raise the matter of the trip with the SENCO in passing. I wanted to hear what exactly their position was, and their reasons for it. I had wanted to meet with the SENCO in any event to discuss the issue of whether Amadi's support assistant would attend the training provided by the learning centre, and so I would ask for information about the trip at the same time.

At the start of Amadi's final week at the learning centre, I had heard nothing further from the SENCO following an email I had sent to her the previous week concerning the training course for the support assistant, so I decided to go into school with Amadi that afternoon and meet with her.

The SENCO told me that she had been away from the office and so had not had a chance to consider the training for Amadi's support assistant. I reminded her that the training was being held that week and that it was unlikely that there would be another opportunity for such training for another year. She confirmed that she had received details of the seminars directly from the learning centre, and the matter was left at that.

Regarding the school trip, without missing a beat, the SENCO told me that neither I nor Amadi was informed because we were not around when the letters went out during the preceding month. She said that it had merely been an oversight but that it was doubtful that there were any more places left. She said she would check the situation and get back to me.

I left the meeting knowing no more than when I went in. We must have spent a good half an hour discussing those two issues but I felt none the wiser for it. I was beginning to discover that saying rather a lot while saying nothing at all was quite clearly a fine art to be cultivated.

By Amadi's last scheduled day at the learning centre, I had still not received her formal Statement of Special Educational

Needs from SENAS. This was over two weeks since the meeting at their office. Until I received the finalized version, I could not appeal against its contents. This of course ensured that Amadi had to conclude her sessions at the learning centre with no idea of whether or not she would return there to continue her journey to becoming a proficient reader.

CHAPTER TWENTY-SEVEN

Exhausting Due Process

The further amendments to Amadi's proposed statutory Statement of Special Educational Needs eventually arrived some weeks later. I went through the document with a fine tooth comb and was thoroughly dismayed to note that nothing at all had been changed, despite the authority being made well aware of their legal requirements in the preparation of this extremely important statutory document. In short, the main parts were exceptionally vague and non-specific to Amadi's needs, despite her detailed, complex cognitive needs. There was no indication of the areas of need such as literacy and numeracy, nor the methods in which she was to be taught, or what they hoped would be achieved. This was all basic stuff which in itself was a clear breach of the relevant law.

The appeals process allowed for a Formal Reconsideration, an internal review, for which I promptly applied, fully pointing out the omissions and their legal duties as far as the detail of the Statement was concerned, before any legal proceedings could be instituted. However, notwithstanding my detailed remonstrations, the Statement was not further amended in any meaningful way; therefore, the only option left open to me was to begin formal legal proceedings at the Special Educational Needs and Disability Tribunal.

This is the stage at which, I know from experience, many parents go no further in their pursuit of justice for their children with cognitive learning difficulties, for varying reasons based on their individual circumstances. Indeed, I definitely knew that this was a monumental step for me to take, which would consume a great deal of my life for a very, very long time. However, save for doing nothing at all, I had no other choice but to press ahead with the legal appeal against their purported, formal Statement.

The task ahead was daunting. Given my dire financial circumstances, I certainly could not afford to retain a specialist educational needs lawyer to represent us. Nor was I eligible for any kind of financial aid. Clearly, my only option was to conduct the case myself. Given my legal background, at least I was some way ahead of the vast majority of parents and caregivers whom simply would not know where to start in such a situation. Apparently, therefore, I was actually one of the lucky ones!

It has been said that a lawyer that represents herself has a fool for a client. Technically, however, I would not be representing myself; I would be representing my daughter. This, to my mind, added a certain poignancy to the situation. After all, in a previous life, I was a tenacious legal advocate, taking on corporations and multi-nationals. I knew that, despite my specialty not being in Special Educational Needs and Disability law and practice, it was an area in which I would have to further submerge myself; and I also knew that representing my daughter meant that I would be as determined as ever to leave no stone unturned.

Once I began my legal research, I came across a few cases where the child themselves had brought cases in proceedings called Judicial Reviews. These were processes whereby the High Court would hear cases where public bodies were challenged for not meeting or exceeding, their statutory powers where it was believed by an individual that a particular decision made by the public body was **unlawful, unreasonable**, or simply **unfair** in the circumstances of their particular case.

I looked into this possibility in a bit more depth in the hope that Amadi **could** be the one to receive the much needed financial assistance. I was referred by a friend to a specialist lawyer who agreed to an initial consultation without charge. Unfortunately, it turned out that this was not a route that could result in any financial aid in Amadi's name directly. However, a legal letter was dispatched to the education authority, free of charge, in the hope that they would further reconsider their position and their continuing duty to provide Amadi with the specific, lawful assistance that she clearly needed, i.e. an **appropriate** education, without the need for any court proceedings.

Unfortunately, even this measure fell on deaf ears in that the education authority would not be moved to make any further adjustments to the official Statement, despite its unlawful vagueness. Clearly, it seemed that due process was the only way forward. I needed to prepare myself mentally, emotionally and physically for the trials that we faced ahead.

The starting point was the legal definition of Special Educational Needs – the special educational provision that was reasonably required, with the focus on Amadi's particular brain function. It did not have to be the best or optimum available, but it had to be "*appropriate*" for **her** particular needs. I contended that it was a reasonable requirement to ensure that Amadi could acquire the most crucial aspect of education, i.e. to be able to **READ**. To date, the mainstream education sector had claimed that they were unable to teach her this fundamental human skill; therefore, she would need to go to a facility that thrived on accomplishing this basic function for children with alternative learning needs.

That in a nutshell was my case. Surely it could not be reasonable to expect Amadi **not** to be able to learn to read where there were established processes to achieve this basic necessity? Surely it was better for Amadi to achieve some level of independence, rather than spending a lifetime dependent on the state? Apparently not, according to the Head of the local education authority's Special Educational Needs and Assessment Service; it certainly was a reasonable expectation, as she had emphatically stated that, "Reading is not a necessity" for my daughter…

CHAPTER TWENTY-EIGHT

Preparations for Legal Proceedings

The starting point for my preparations was to be clear about what the law around compulsory education actually was, and then to satisfy myself on the requirements around the provision for children with special educational needs and disabilities.

In the first instance, it is clear that it is the duty of **the parent** to secure an efficient, full time education that is suitable to the age, ability and aptitude of their children, and to secure any **continuing** special educational need he or she may have. I'm sure that not many parents have any idea that this is actually **THEIR** responsibility!

This is to be achieved, either by regular attendance at a school **or otherwise**, so long as this does not incur **unreasonable** public expenditure. Emphatically, it is a legal duty of the education authority to **promote** the education of ALL of the people within their environs, whether that is within their own schools **or elsewhere**, in consultation with the child's parent! The law is absolutely clear on this point; indeed, the provision could even be in another country, with a companion, to attend an institution which specializes in providing for children with special educational needs! Who knew? I did, and that is precisely why I was so resolute in pursuing my daughter's lawful entitlement to an education appropriate to *her* particular needs.

So far as the actual official Statement of Special Educational Needs was concerned, the law states that it **SHALL** specify the special educational provision to be made for the purpose of meeting those particular needs, including *any other institution* which would be appropriate for the child (presumably if the authority themselves contend that they cannot meet them). It is incumbent upon **the parent** to ensure that these arrangements are made; if they don't, then the education authority *must*. These provisions must of course first be specified in the Statement of Special Educational Needs. It is precisely due to the absence of these provisions in that document that the legal proceedings became necessary.

Once I had clarified these fundamental tenets of my claim, I began to draft our SEN Appeal Form, ensuring that I included all of the necessary documents and correspondence which evidenced our legitimate reasons for appealing the education authority's flawed decision.

Over the next few months, evidence was sought from the Williams Syndrome Foundation, an eminent Professor who had conducted and documented numerous research studies into the needs of people with Williams Syndrome and the type of learning instruction that they required, a government sponsored report into the learning needs of cognitively challenged children and their learning needs, Amadi's specialist learning center, and numerous case law reports. I ensured that our case was meticulously evidenced whilst outlining the deficiencies in the local education authority's position which focused on their teaching *strategy* rather than Amadi's learning ability – her cognition. They were trying to make her (and others) learn by rote with no understanding whatsoever, instead of adopting or utilizing sensory-cognitive learning measures for reading, comprehension and numeracy, as they do very effectively at the learning centre.

The completed appeal forms were duly dispatched to the tribunal with a note of our only witness – the learning centre's London Director. She had agreed to attend to articulate and explain the concept imagery and cognitive-sensory method of learning which the local education authority had to date failed to grasp. She was also to emphasize the fact that this method did not have to be at one of their centers; it could be learned by a school teacher who could then teach it in mainstream school!

The Director would be explaining to the tribunal that Amadi had begun to take pride in her reading endeavors; her "I don't knows" were far less in number than when she began a few weeks past. Her 'learned helplessness' had completely gone – she had developed the courage to take risks instead of to withdraw. Amadi had achieved *a year and four months* worth of growth in just a few weeks. Her focus had improved exponentially and she was at a fragile stage where the intensive instruction needed to be continued.

The Director was to emphasize that Amadi was nowhere near where she should have been as a ten year old (given her time in mainstream education), but there had been vast improvements – Amadi's neurons were at last being activated!

CHAPTER TWENTY-NINE

The Hearing: Equal before the Law?

As a matter of procedure, the tribunal had stipulated that each side had a limit of two witnesses. However, the education authority had proffered three – their Principal Educational Psychologist, their "SEN Consultant," and the school's SEN Coordinator. They had also requested that the school's Head Teacher be allowed to sit in – I refused this request as I felt that enough was enough! Plus, they had a lawyer and Counsel representing them.

I represented my daughter myself, and the Director of the learning centre agreed to attend on our behalf to explain the importance of the sensory-cognitive method of learning. I consider it so sad that the local education authority was clearly very happy to spend an inordinate amount of financial resources in *resisting* our plea to properly educate my daughter, when the huge cost of their **defending** our action could so easily have helped Amadi and so many other learning disabled children within their authority to simply *learn* to read. The concept of Equality of Alms was sadly lacking in these proceedings. The fact that I had a legal background undoubtedly helped us enormously; but, what of the parents who do not have this purported 'advantage…'? By the date of the hearing I'd left no stone unturned and was exceptionally prepared for the battle that lay ahead.

The day began by me introducing Amadi to the judges, lest they forget that we were dealing with a living being and not just a statistic. They questioned her gently about school but she was too frightened to respond. The panel reassured her that all was okay, after which she told them that she enjoyed being with her friends, but didn't like it when the School's Special Educational Needs Coordinator shouted at her. This surprised even me and I asked her about when that happens. She responded that it was when she didn't understand something that she was asked. I glanced at the SENCO who turned a very bright color of red. Moving on, I asked Amadi to tell the panel how she felt about the learning centre. She visibly brightened and said that she loved learning to read! After a few minutes, I took her to a private room where she could entertain herself on her electronic tablet while the hearing continued in her absence.

After I introduced our appeal, I stressed that I had tried for many years to get the school to adopt appropriate learning processes *within the school* for a great many of their pupils, including Amadi, without success; after which I had to turn to the private sector. The evidential basis for Amadi's learning requirements were presented in the form of several research studies led by renowned Professors, including *'Learning to Read in Williams Syndrome: Looking Beneath the Surface of Atypical Reading Development'* (2001), and *'Research into Williams Syndrome: The State of the Art'* (2008), Annette Karmiloff-Smith. They provided in depth analysis of the unique character of the brain function of people with Williams Syndrome (and some on the Autistic Spectrum), and the vital importance of cognition in their learning/ability to learn. Essentially, there are "serious deficits" in cognition and their brain processes, which requires the cognitive-sensory connection to language in their understanding of literacy and math.

I then called our witness, the Director of the learning center. After explaining the importance of the cognitive-sensory approach to learning as opposed to the school's strategy based teaching, she then told of how Amadi's overall reading development had improved exponentially. Amadi's "I don't knows" were far less than before, and she was taking pride in endeavoring to read; her 'learned helplessness' had gone completely – she now had the courage to take risks instead of withdrawing; a year and four months' worth of growth had been achieved in just a few weeks. The Director stipulated that it was essential for the intensive instruction to continue, as Amadi had acquired an improved focus and was now at a fragile place.

The Director stressed that Amadi was nowhere near where she should be as a 10 year old (given her formative years in mainstream primary education), but she had made vast improvements, as they were now going beneath the surface and Amadi's neurons were being activated by her new found ability to learn. Amadi was developing concept imagery skills and the essential foundations were now being built. The learning centre had noticed favorable attitude changes in her, as she displayed far less frustration than when she had begun at their facility.

The education authority's Counsel then put their case through their witnesses. In essence, they claimed that they didn't have the space or resources to provide the type of instruction that Amadi was said to require, and, they use the multi-sensory approach for very young children and it had worked very well.

They claimed that the external provision at the learning centre could not be continued as they considered it an inefficient use of public resources. The judges asked pertinent questions around the Cognitive-Sensory approach and it became abundantly clear that not one of them had any understanding at all of this different type of learning instruction, and they assumed that it was the same as *multi-sensory*. I assisted the judge by referring to a Government sponsored report which acknowledged that the State system does not know *how* to treat "this kind of cognitive deficiency" – *Identifying and Teaching Children and Young People with Dyslexia and Literacy Difficulties – An independent report from Sir Jim Rose to the Secretary of State for Children, Schools and Families, June 2009*. It clearly recognised the different approach that was required.

Multi-sensory, I explained was dealing with the five senses of touch, smell, sight, taste and hearing – feelings, not knowledge. The cognitive-sensory approach, on the other hand, relates to and deals with the **brain** and how it first receives and processes information. There is a profound and distinct difference which is fundamental to the learning processes of many children who are consistently failed by the education system.

The school's Special Educational Needs Co-ordinator was openly reluctant to assist in finding any sort of middle ground, but the education authority's "SEN Consultant" clearly became more interested in finding out more about this alternative method of helping these cognitively challenged pupils to actually *learn*. This was a major step! She went further to suggest an appropriately qualified individual could be found to provide what was required *within the school*!

I reminded the judges that the law required that the provision be made "otherwise than in a school" where it was clear that the school could not meet the educational need. If that was really the case (which I doubted), I would be happy for Amadi to continue attending half a day in school and half a day at the learning centre, but the detail of the provision had by law to be ensconced within her statutory Statement.

After two extended days of the hearing and submissions, the judges adjourned to consider their final decision which was to be sent to the parties within a few weeks. It was over. Totally exhausted, we returned home and life went on as we waited to find out how the next stage of Amadi's learning was to continue.

CHAPTER THIRTY

The Conclusion –
and Personal Sadness

One afternoon some weeks later as we settled into a new year, there was a loud thud as the postman made his delivery. The Decision had arrived. I picked up the large, thick envelope bearing the Tribunal's stamp and just held it for a while. I took it into my kitchen, sat down and placed the envelope on the table. I stared at it for several minutes, wondering what the Decision was and how our immediate future would be impacted by it. My heart began to race and I decided that a glass of wine was definitely required in order to calm my nerves prior to the grand reveal.

Some twenty minutes later, I was ready. I slowly opened the package, removed the bundle which consisted of some twenty-eight pages, and began to read. I was determined to get through all of the stated Appeal against the contents of Amadi's Statement of Educational Needs, the full Facts of the two day hearing and then the Conclusions with Reasons before going through the actual Order that had been made. The Decision was certainly very thorough and an impressive read, with the tribunal stating precisely what had to be included within Amadi's Statement, and the wording which had to be used.

We'd done it! The Statement had to be substantially revised to include the specificity required by law tailored to Amadi's particular, appropriate needs. The cognitive-sensory method of learning had to be utilized by an appropriately qualified teacher and, based on what had been recognized towards the end of the hearing, the teaching had to be provided within the school! It wasn't considered necessary for Amadi to have to access the appropriate learning processes by attending at the learning centre when it was not *inappropriate* for her to access them in school. Therefore, after my many years of pleading for this precise outcome, it had now been ordered as a matter of law! I breathed a great sigh of relief and polished off my glass of wine. The judgment would now serve as a legal precedent for others with similar issues and concerns – provided of course that they have the endurance, tenacity and persistence to keep on going year after year, after year, taking on the might of the system which could simply be too daunting for many. I sincerely hope that this judgment will also serve as a catalyst for change.

Amadi's story demonstrates quite graphically how the vast majority of our children with additional learning needs are simply not afforded that to which they are lawfully entitled within the state education system. My daughter has become a proficient reader as I promised her that she would. That is because I was able to advocate for her to ensure that ***the missing link*** between education and learning, given her cognitive understanding, was finally connected to reveal her ***Special Hidden Talents***.

Governmental Update

In 2018, the government announced new action to improve outcomes for children with additional needs, while warning that the funding shortfall for children with special educational needs and disabilities (SEND) must be urgently addressed.

The Deputy Chair of London Councils said: "The number of pupils with complex needs in London has increased significantly in recent years, and this trend is set to continue. We're urging the government to review funding allocations to make sure schools across the capital are able to meet the needs of their most vulnerable pupils."

Epilogue

My elation over our monumental success soon turned to abject sadness. Two months prior to the hearing, the only other person in the whole world who cared about us and the outcome of our long battles had passed away. My father, Amadi's grandfather was our only emotional support. He had provided us with unconditional love and support since Amadi's birth and he was a great source of encouragement through all of our trials and tribulations. We had/have no other support. In tribute to him, I wrote the following on the day he passed, and after we attended his burial:-

Ode to my Dad who passed on
7th September, 2009, aged 83 years and 28 days:
My Daddy, My Hero

You raised us up in such difficult circumstances.
You encouraged us and made us believe
that all of our dreams were possible.
You showed us, by example, how to do
well, aim high and never give up.
You made us feel safe and secure when,
I grew to know, times were so very hard.
You protected us when we felt vulnerable.
You did your very best when, as I grew
to know, you were acting alone.
You made us know in our souls that
the world was our oyster.
You instilled in us an unshakeable belief in ourselves.

You provided Amadi and me with the love,
support and encouragement that only my Daddy knew how.
You gave me hope when it seemed that none was left.
You were my beacon of light in a sometimes
harsh and unfriendly world.
You were full of knowledge and inspiration
which you gladly imparted.
You lifted me up when I felt as though
circumstances and situations had let me down.
You held on until your only son arrived to be with you
so he could say goodbye, in person, from all of us.
I know in my heart that you managed to do this to
ensure that our grief would be somehow bearable.
Thank you, Daddy. You were, you are
and will always be, my hero.
"Chi girl"

****

Farewell Daddy!
14-Dec-2009

We have now returned from my father's burial and I feel that I can now move on, buoyed by the thought of closure and renewal as I move on in what for me is a new and changed world.

My Dad's burial was extremely emotional and phenomenally spectacular! The proceedings ran over 3 days – the procession with Daddy in his casket, the ceremonies – both Christian and traditional, culminating in the physical burial, and then the celebration procession which saw us walking many miles through the various villages acknowledging the love and condolences from, what seemed to me, everyone in the entire State! What a way to go – my Dad was clearly much loved and has left a wonderful legacy. He would have loved every minute of it.

There was a hilarious episode while my Dad was being buried where I was sobbing uncontrollably, and then the lead digger stopped proceedings with a flourish of his spade and demanded that a crate of Guinness and a bottle of gin be secured immediately, lest Daddy got thirsty! It was absolutely bizarre and left me laughing uncontrollably through my tears! Just the type of thing Daddy would have done!

It was surreal and fabulous and wonderful, and I am so grateful that Amadi and I were there to say goodbye in that very public, spectacular way. And now we go on with the rest of our lives, without him.

★★★★★★★★★★

About the Author

A Corporate Lawyer who spent over 20 years leading teams of lawyers and other professionals, Chineme studied for many post graduate diplomas, including an MBA with the Open University, had Directorships at Lawyers in Local Government Ltd and Special Hidden Talents Ltd, and is a member of the Chartered Institute of Managers. As a woman working in a male-dominated corporate world for over 20 years, Chineme realised early on that it was essential for her to be able to deal effectively with the ongoing challenges and opportunities with which her rapid career progression inevitably presented. Chineme's daughter has cognitive learning difficulties and her past experiences served her well in dealing with the challenges and opportunities that her daughter faced within the education system.

Chineme is now an internet entrepreneur, success coach and author who believes that success is not just about the finances; more importantly, it is about taking responsibility for our own futures, right now. Chineme helps people to overcome the very real problems they face which can overwhelm and rob them of their well-being and happiness. She does this by dealing effectively with what she refers to as the mountains and molehills that we all encounter in our daily lives. In one of her published works, *There Is No Time Like the Present to Create Your Future*, Chineme formulated seven action steps in order that anybody can take charge of their present to create for themselves a better future. They are action steps that will change attitudes and, indeed, people's lives.

Chineme is available for seminars, retreats and speaking engagements. Email: *hello@specialhiddentalents.com*

9 781999 679507